THE State of Affairs

"Affairs are seldom understood. Todd Mulliken explains who and why."
—LEITH ANDERSON, Pastor of Wooddale Church
Eden Prairie, Minnesota

"This book is for couples who want to take their relationship to the ultimate level of satisfaction."
—Pianist LORIE LINE

"In a culture increasingly defined by the breakdown of marriage and the proliferation of adulterous affairs, this is a timely and enormously helpful book. Not only is Todd's depiction of the personality types and behaviors of those involved in affairs right on target, but his specific recommendations for healing, recovery, and . . . life change are both insightful and realistic."
—JEFF SIEMON, former Minnesota Vikings All-Pro Linebacker
Current Director of Search Ministries and Straight Talk
(A group dedicated to helping men live lives of integrity)

"Are you a pleaser or a controller? You will understand yourself and your spouse better when you read this book. And you may save your marriage from the anguish of an affair."
—GAYLEN CALL, Senior Pastor of Grace Church
Roseville, Minnesota

"In a world obsessed with personal fulfillment, extramarital affairs are as common and prolific as weeds in a garden. How can we stop this trend? It starts with understanding ourselves and the conditions that set us up for affairs. From his practical experience as a therapist, Todd Mulliken has the insight you need to affair-proof and strengthen your marriage."
—DR. JAY M. ZINN, author of The Unveiling

TODD MULLIKEN

THE STATE OF AFFAIRS

WHY THEY HAPPEN & HOW LOVE CAN BE RESTORED

WINEPRESS WP PUBLISHING

ISBN 1-57921-113-5
Library of Congress Catalog Card Number: 98-60451

Acknowledgments

So many people have been supportive of this effort. Without question, my wife, Laura, and our three daughters have been gracious and encouraging throughout the process. My good friends and editors, Ed and Anne Stych, have been selfless and completely available to help with the project from beginning to end. A dear friend of my father and myself, Dr. James Bell, author and historian, has been a fabulous mentor and a voice of reason. Dr. Phil and Mary Olson have openly given of their time and resources. My family of origin—Mom, Dad, and sister Trudi—also have been strong voices of support. My colleagues at my clinic, Dr. Bill Harley, and the hundreds of friends and members of our church also have been an inspiration to me in completing this book. Thank you and Godspeed to you all.

Table of Contents

Foreword

꧁꧂

A famous actor during a television interview celebrated his long marriage to his beautiful wife. The reporter challenged the actor, saying, "How do you manage to stay married to one person against all of the temptations and pressures that the two of you face?"

The actor replied, "In my family, growing up, we were taught that if something was broken, we should fix it—not throw it away." His voice seems a lonely one given the much-trumpeted view of the short-term, easy-come-easy-go relational world mirrored by the Hollywood mystique.

When I was given the privilege of writing the foreword to *The State of Affairs*, the actor's comments came to my mind immediately. This wonderful, practical handbook is a much-needed voice in rebuilding marriages that are broken, as well as preventive medicine for many marriages that could end up shattered because the couple is flirting with discarding their vows and commitments.

Todd Mulliken's practical clinical experience challenges the mentality that our feelings at any one moment—toward our spouse or our partner in an affair—should determine our choices. He carefully and gently suggests that our values and what people really want from their lives is a much better lens through which we should view life-changing decisions. In my profession as a minister, I see this book as a cry of hope in a wilderness of confusion and despair.

This book also does not assume that all affairs have been created equal. Wrapping them in story form, Todd clearly outlines the patterns, types, and levels of extramarital affairs. Todd does an excellent job of connecting past family dynamics to present marital relationships and extramarital activity. So many of those I have encountered have no concept of how their current extramarital behavior connects with their other relationships, let alone how it is grounded in past ways of coping within family systems. Anyone who is fighting with this problem or knows someone who is will want to read or recommend this book.

This book offers concrete suggestions to individuals on both sides of a broken marriage. Todd gives couples a roadmap out of their current situation and back to a healthy, long-term marriage. Therapists, pastors, couples, and friends now have a tool to facilitate renewal in broken relationships.

DAVID STARK
Author of *Life Keys*
Pastor, Christ Presbyterian Church
Edina, Minnesota

Chapter One
Understanding Affairs

༺༻

I f, as the song says, there are fifty ways to leave your lover, then there are at least as many reasons why millions of happily married American couples eventually end up divorced.

Sudden job loss. Physical abuse. The death of a child. Alcohol or drug abuse. Money problems. Even the subtle pressure from modern society to look out for oneself first has led countless couples into despair and eventual divorce.

But the single greatest threat to any marriage is adultery. Recent studies show that 65 percent of married couples who experience an affair end up divorced.

Think about that. For every one hundred couples who go through an affair, sixty five can't recover from the hurt and anger and end up leaving the person they promised to "love and hold forever." No other pressure in a marriage comes close to the emotional devastation of an affair.

But there's hope. If a man and woman know how to deal with adultery, should it occur, there's a great chance they can end the affair and restore love to their marriage. Fewer than 5 percent of the couples I counsel end up divorced. If the affair ends promptly after the spouse discovers it, fewer than 1 percent of the people I work with go to divorce court.

I have succeeded in helping couples recover from affairs because I don't believe in treating every adulterous relationship the same way. I have identified the five most common extramarital affairs in society today and have developed specific treatments based on the type of affair.

In this book, I dedicate a chapter to each of the five types of affairs, demonstrating them with real-life examples from my years of clinical work. There's also a chapter on a new kind of affair, one that is bound to be in the top five by the turn of the century: the Cyber Affair. I show how I helped each of the six couples end the affair and move on to healing and restoring their marriages. In the final two chapters, I discuss in more detail the healing and reconciliation process and how couples can prevent infidelity from ever disrupting their lives. But before moving on to the case studies, let's talk in general about who has affairs and why.

Why Women Have Affairs
A woman generally has an affair because she is lonely and unhappy with her marriage. It's rare that a happily married woman engages in infidelity. Women invest a lot of who they are in marriage, so when a woman has received a moderate or high level of fulfillment in her marital life, she will likely avoid the traps that lead to infidelity.

Married women who are vulnerable to affairs are typically nurturing, sensitive, caring, and passive. They are also tired, emotionally bankrupt, and incredibly lonely. They commit an act of desperation—the affair—that everyone who knows them would not expect based on the woman's values and integrity. This type of woman accounts for 90 percent of married women who have affairs. It's essential for men married to this type of woman to be sensitive to their needs.

The remaining 10 percent of women who have affairs are aggressive, impulsive, and seductive. Typically, this kind of woman is unmarried and is involved with a married man. Married women of this type are usually vulnerable to an affair because they were spoiled as children. When they want to have an affair, they ask themselves, "Why can't I have this, too?" If this type of woman has an affair, it has little to do with her marriage. Instead, it's a symptom of her character. Occasionally, women like this struggle with a severe personality problem or a form of mental illness that impairs their ability to be stable in marriage. Their upbringing may have been abusive and chaotic, and they are simply repeating the pattern of self-destruction that they saw growing up.

What About Men?

Men who have struggled with intimacy their entire lives are most vulnerable to infidelity. During childhood, they learn behaviors from their families that leave them incapable of loving themselves and others, especially within marital and family life.

This type of man often develops a double life. At home, he is emotionally uninvolved and distant, while at work or play he becomes "successful" through addiction to work, sports, or the endearment of women. This type of man accounts for 80 percent of the married men who have affairs.

The passive male accounts for the other 20 percent. Contrary to the Double-Life Man, the Passive Man usually has an affair because of marital dissatisfaction. He eventually becomes vulnerable to an aggressive, seductive woman who pursues him. He will occasionally be involved with a Passive Woman. The Passive Man has a hard time getting out of the affair at first, but once he is out, he rarely returns to the pattern of infidelity. On the other hand, the Double-Life Man will continue with this pattern until he comes to grips with some significant past and present emotional problems in his life.

Men have always struggled with monogamy, lust, and their desire to "sow their seed" with different women. But the good news is that these tendencies can be controlled. Over the last two generations, millions of men have learned how to nurture, have become more intimate with their wives and families, and have become committed to fidelity in their marriage. The men who can do this also pass on a great gift to their sons: the capacity to love, nurture, and be committed to marital life and fidelity.

Do Personalities Play a Factor?

Everyone falls into one of two basic personality categories: Controllers and Pleasers. Controllers often have leadership roles in their work lives and are directive, hard working, spontaneous, and focused; yet they struggle with being impulsive, self-centered, argumentative, and strong willed. In addition, Controllers sometimes have a history of boundary problems in their relationships with the opposite sex.

Controllers develop their personality based on one of the following types of upbringing:

1. They may have grown up in a healthy home where they tended to get their own way. They were driven, successful, and encountered few struggles in life. They control as adults because they tend to be in charge and have been fortunate in making decisions that have helped them do well.
2. Often, however, they are raised in a controlling, somewhat chaotic environment in which many fears and a lack of intimacy are the norm.

Controllers internalize a great deal of anger during this phase of their life, and they spend the rest of their adulthood expressing this anger toward others. The controlling aspect of their personality becomes more apparent through the insecurity they feel in intimate environments, such as their family life.

The Pleaser is blessed with a nurturing and accommodating spirit, the ability to be a consistent and steadfast friend, the ability to be a good team player in work and family life, and the ability to be a great listener. But Pleasers are passive and avoid conflict, are easily controlled, tend to internalize their emotions, and lack direction for themselves.

Pleasers develop their personality based on one of the following scenarios:

1. Their upbringing may have been generally healthy. Their family probably had the ability to serve each other in love and to resolve conflict lovingly. The capability to nurture and love was established and maintained.
2. They may have grown up in an unhealthy family system of control in which they were shut down and rarely allowed to tell their own story. They developed the role of listener. The

ability to listen is an admirable trait, but it also makes them easily controlled in marital and family life. Sometimes they never have a chance to speak about their own issues.

It's important to recognize the power that personality plays in infidelity. About 60 percent of affairs occur between people of similar personalities. These people often believe fate has drawn them together and that they are soul mates. They also believe this other person is so much different from the person they married that they must have married the wrong person.

In an affair between two Controllers, the relationship will be stormy, chaotic, and full of turmoil. But because they're used to this kind of intensity, they feel it must be fate. These affairs are typically short-lived and are sometimes abusive.

When two Pleasers get together, the attraction is that there is no conflict, no arguing, no intense discussion. There is rarely a decision made, but the two passive people don't care. They'll do whatever it takes to avoid conflict. This type of affair can go on and on but seldom does it ever cause marriages to break up. The partners are just two victims consoling each other about their miserable lives.

An emotional affair can consist of either two Controllers or two Pleasers. This type of affair may not include sex, so it doesn't have the strength of sexual involvement attached. The allure in this affair is the positive, and sometimes seductive, interactions between the individuals, as well as the fantasy of what the relationship might become.

Two Controllers usually won't wait long to add sex to their relationship, but two Pleasers might wait years. Controllers will follow through on their impulses because they are decisive, while Pleasers are sometimes too indecisive to follow through on their drives.

The remaining 40 percent of affairs occur between people of different personalities. They are often duplicating the same relationship they have in their marriage. For example, the Lonely Woman may be drawn into an affair by a strong, loving man who begins to control her after a period of time, just as her husband has for years. In the case of the Passive Man, he may be drawn into an affair by a dominant woman whose personality is similar to his wife's. At first he's trapped by her seductive ways, but eventually he becomes controlled, just as he is by his wife.

Where Affairs Typically Begin

More than 70 percent of affairs start in the workplace. People frequently feel good about their identities at work making them more likely to cross boundaries emotionally and sexually. Also, the workplace can provide secrecy and passion, two things on which affairs thrive.

Much of a man's identity and self-image comes from his job, so men are more easily drawn into affairs at work because of the power, status, and self-confidence they feel. Women are equally subject to affairs in the workplace, but it's only since they have become more involved in working outside the home over the last three decades that extramarital affairs of this type have increased. Often, the workplace offers an environment in which there are no boundaries in terms of interpersonal relationships. A Lonely Woman, for instance, may be drawn to a male co-worker who treats her with respect and admires her abilities, while at home she is unloved and mistreated by her husband. The Double-Life Man may have multiple affairs at work because it adds passion and purpose to his life, and it's a consistent boost to his ego. But at home he repeats the pattern of isolation and nonintimacy he experienced as a child.

The remaining 30 percent of affairs occur in situations outside work, most involving longtime friends who engage in an emotional relationship that often leads to a powerful sexual affair. It's likely that the people involved in this type of affair are either both Controllers or both Pleasers.

I have also counseled cases in which high school reunions— especially the ten and twenty year reunions—produce an affair between old sweethearts. This type of affair is sparked by memories and usually dwindles over time, but it's particularly dangerous because of future reunions. Other types of outside-of-work affairs occur in social environments such as support groups, bars, churches, and community organizations. They even occur on the Internet.

Is It Time for an Affair?

I have counseled hundreds of people who say they are experiencing the same type of marriage as their parents did. Growing up, they watched their parents stay in hopeless and unfulfilling marriages, and they're adamant that they're not going to have the same kind of life. Their answer tends to be to run away or to run into someone else's arms.

More than 60 percent of affairs occur after ten years of marriage. Affairs often take this long to develop because it takes years for unhealthy and unfulfilling patterns to settle into a marriage. Couples struggle with these patterns as they develop, then become resigned to them when they don't disappear.

The only type of affair that occurs early in marriage is the case of the Double-Life Man. This man sometimes has an affair early in marriage because of the commitment problems he has had with women since adolescence and because of his lack of emotional involvement in his marital life. It is often the case with the Double-Life Man that his wife doesn't learn of his exploits until years later. The longer this man stays in his pattern of infidelity, the longer it may take his wife to forgive him.

Defining an Affair

Affairs aren't just about sex. When any relationship with the opposite sex affects the level of intimacy, emotional closeness, and commitment of a marriage, you've crossed the line to an extramarital affair. While a sexual relationship clearly strengthens an affair and makes it more difficult to break off, an emotional affair can also cause irreparable damage to a marriage.

Names and cities in the following case studies are fictional for the purpose of confidentiality and clients' rights.

Chapter Two
The Lonely Woman

⟨✹⟩

About 25 percent of my infidelity cases involve the Lonely Woman. It is the most difficult affair to break off, mostly because the woman is indecisive, the man she is having the affair with begins to control her, and she has been unhappy with her marriage for such a long time. This is the story of Linda, a thirty-six year old who typifies the Lonely Woman.

PROFILE: LINDA THE LISTENER

Linda grew up in a Detroit suburb as the middle child of three. She was a good listener who often showed concern for other people. But like a lot of caring listeners, she didn't talk much about herself with her parents, friends, or boyfriends.

Linda's parents had a distant marriage. They argued a lot and rarely showed each other affection in public. In her family life, Linda was controlled by her mother. Linda listened closely to her, whether it was about complaints with life or about what chore needed to be done next. Linda spent little time with her father.

"Whenever he talked to me, it was about school or family matters or to discipline me," Linda said. "He was at work most of the time anyway. He often worked into the night."

Linda's relationships with her brother and sister and childhood friends were good. She was a consistent friend who listened to their concerns and asked about their lives. In her dating relationships, she also was a listener who was controlled by her boyfriends' moods. She did everything she could to help her boyfriends and take care of their concerns.

A Marriage in Crisis: Who's in Control?

Linda was twenty-two when she married Steve, a man she had dated for about eighteen months.

"Steve is a lot like my dad in that he works a lot," Linda said. "Steve also spends a lot of time playing sports and staying out late with his friends. There never seems to be time for me except when he's in the mood for sex. We'll go out occasionally, but even then he would rather talk to other people than to me. Even though he's not home a lot, he still runs the show, deciding how to spend our money and time. I usually just go along. I don't always agree, but I'd rather not rock the boat."

Linda is controlled by Steve just as she was controlled by her mother. She's controlled by his moods, his decisions, his opinions. Feeling unloved by Steve, Linda began growing disenchanted with her life shortly after the birth of their second child when Linda was twenty-eight.

Eventually, the family was unable to live on Steve's salary alone, so Linda took a job in the customer-service department of a large company. The job was a good fit for her giving, caring personality. She made friends with co-workers and customers quickly and received accolades for her work. Both Steve and their children supported her decision to work outside the home. Steve liked the extra money, and the children liked that she seemed happier.

"I had a lot of demands at home, and I sometimes felt overworked," Linda said. "But I really enjoyed my job. Taking that job also opened my eyes to what was going on with me and my marriage. I began to reflect more on my life."

What she saw was a woman who lacked direction and confidence. She also saw a woman who had slowly become dissatisfied with her marriage of thirteen years. Steve was controlling, sexually demanding, and unappreciative of her efforts to raise their children. She saw a woman who resembled her mother. This thought haunted Linda.

She Meets a Man Who Cares

Joe had been a respected manager for many years with Linda's company. Linda first talked at length with him following a regular department meeting. They spent two hours alone talking about the company. Linda was impressed that Joe seemed strong, yet kind, but she was especially struck that he showed genuine interest in her opinions.

At the next department meeting four days later, Joe sat next to Linda and greeted her fondly. After the meeting, Joe invited Linda to join him and three colleagues for lunch. She agreed, but only reluctantly, because she knew the other people only superficially. Later that afternoon, Joe stopped by Linda's office and thanked her for going to lunch. Linda was surprised by his visit and found herself embarrassed and nervous, but Joe's calm, confident way comforted her as they chatted briefly about company issues.

"I feel like I barely know you," Joe said. "Tell me a little bit about your family."

Linda talked about Steve and the children. Joe said he was separated from his wife, and a divorce looked inevitable.

"I was surprised that a man with his kindness and confidence would be in the midst of a divorce," Linda said. "But his wife apparently had emotional problems that he had difficulty dealing with."

Joe thanked Linda for her interest and said he would like to learn more about her life sometime. Linda said she would like that.

This was the start of Linda's affair. Joe and Linda, both at points in their lives where they were vulnerable and in need of attention, had crossed the boundary separating work and personal life.

"I thought about Joe constantly that night," Linda said. "I couldn't believe how close I felt to him in such a short period of time. I had never met a man who seemed so vulnerable and caring. I knew my feelings weren't right, but I still felt good about Joe."

Two days later, Joe stopped by Linda's office and asked her to lunch. She eagerly agreed and looked forward to spending time with this other man. After talking about work, Joe apologized for unloading his family situation on Linda but again thanked her for listening and caring. Joe asked more about Linda's family life, and she began to open up about some of her marital problems.

"Joe asked me if Steve and I had sought marital counseling," Linda said. "Steve wasn't interested in that, but Joe encouraged me to at least seek help for myself like he did for himself."

No Longer Just Friends

Linda and Joe began to meet regularly for lunch, and their conversations moved from business to almost exclusively about their marital hardships. Linda began to care a great deal for Joe, and this frightened her. She knew she was crossing the line with him emotionally, but she would not stop.

"I believed that I deserved to feel like that," Linda said. "For the first time in my life, I felt loved and listened to by a man, and there was no sex involved."

Linda's troubles at home escalated. She began to pressure Steve about marriage counseling, but he dismissed her request as a phase and told her to quit complaining. He said they had a good marriage compared with other couples they knew.

At Linda's next department meeting, her group decided to put more time into a lagging marketing project. Joe offered to take over the project but said he needed help accumulating data. Linda said her workload had slowed down and offered to help. To meet the deadline, night and weekend work would be required. Joe offered his apartment as a meeting place if the workplace environment became too stale. Linda knew immediately that the emotional and physical stakes were about to rise.

Linda explained to Steve that she would have to work a couple of weekends and that he would need to be at home for the children. Although Steve had no plans, he was furious that Linda would be away at work.

"At that point, I broke down and cried," Linda said. "Steve didn't even respond. He just left the room. I felt so lost. I didn't feel any love from, or for, Steve, yet I had all these wonderful feelings for Joe."

Linda and Joe met at work at two o'clock Saturday afternoon and planned to work until eight. About four hours later, Joe suggested that they pick up some Chinese food and go back to his apartment where they could wrap up their day's work. Linda entered Joe's apartment with a sense of nervous apprehension. She felt like she was dating again, except this time with the security that she felt so cared for by Joe.

They returned to their research after dinner, but their discussion soon turned personal. They talked for the first time about their feelings for each other. Joe said he struggled with how much he had grown to care for Linda.

"I told Joe that in all my years of marriage, Steve had never respected me as much as he had," Linda said. "I also told him I was very confused about my life and that I was scared about how I felt about him."

Joe then moved closer and embraced Linda for the first time.

"I felt this incredible rush of emotions go through my body," Linda said. "I immediately sank into his arms, and we held each other in silence for several minutes."

Joe said finally that it was seven-thirty and that she should leave so she could be home by eight as scheduled. Linda felt honored that Joe didn't pursue her sexually. Steve only offered affection with sex tied to it. She felt freer with Joe.

The next day, Joe and Linda worked again at the office and talked about their marriages. They embraced again as they left work.

"That night at home I felt miserable," Linda said. "Steve was upset that my job was taking too much time away from the family. And then there were the nasty remarks about not having had sex for the past three weeks."

As Linda's emotions for Joe grew, her hatred for Steve grew as well. She found herself repulsed by his lack of sensitivity and his demands for sex.

"I yelled at him for the first time in years. I told Steve how unhappy I was and that I was going to find a counselor for myself. He just laughed."

On Monday, Linda and Joe went to lunch at a Chinese restaurant that had become their regular rendezvous. Linda started crying during lunch saying that Steve was so hurtful to her that she wanted to leave him but was afraid to do so because of the children. Joe empathized saying he felt the same way about his wife before they separated. Joe said counseling helped him, and he encouraged her to get help. He had also brought Linda a book on healing troubled marriages.

Joe said he looked forward to working on the project during the upcoming weekend just so he could be with her. They laughed together about this, held hands across the table, and looked into each other's eyes as never before. Joe leaned down and kissed Linda's hand gently and said he would be there for her because he cared for her deeply and he knew that she hurt.

From the Boardroom to the Bedroom

Linda awoke Saturday with great anticipation about seeing Joe later that day. Spending time with him was becoming easier. Because Steve wasn't treating her well, her guilt about spending time with Joe had vanished.

When Joe and Linda met at the office that day, Joe appeared tired and sad. Linda immediately embraced him and asked what was wrong. He said his oldest son was arrested for drunken driving the night before and that he felt guilty for not spending enough time with him while he and his wife were separated during the last two years. Joe and Linda spent some time talking about this, then they decided to put off work for a while and go to Joe's apartment to talk.

Linda the listener and giver was in her prime now. Not only was she helping a man, she was also beginning to love him as well.

Once at the apartment, Joe thanked her again for listening so well to his concerns. He leaned over and kissed her gently on the lips. Linda again felt a rush of emotions, and their kiss turned into more kisses. Joe lifted Linda into his arms and carried her into his bedroom where they made love with a passion neither had experienced before.

Over the next four months, Linda and Joe sustained their sexual relationship and continued to see each other outside of work regularly. But Linda became increasingly confused. She was clear about whom she loved and who loved her, but what was she going to do with her life? Making decisions was very difficult for her.

Meanwhile, Steve continued to be Steve: controlling, unloving, and uninvolved emotionally in the marriage. He didn't have a clue about the affair. He knew only that Linda was withdrawn, angry, and working more. Joe declared his love and said he was willing to be with Linda forever, but he didn't pressure her to get out of the marriage.

TREATMENT

Changing Long-Term Patterns

Linda and Steve both must change if they hope to restore their marriage and keep their family intact.

Steve is a typical Controller. He must learn that he can't, and shouldn't try, to control everything in his marriage, and he must learn how to love Linda the way she needs to be loved.

Linda must stop allowing everyone to control her. She must understand why she has been controlled by other people during her entire life and that the affair with Joe would eventually turn into the same kind of relationship. She must also learn how to express herself emotionally with people, especially loved ones. First of all, however, she must end the affair and take responsibility for that mistake. She must not view herself as a victim of circumstances.

Counseling Steve and Linda individually was important to help them understand the specific changes each had to make. Individual counseling can last from three to six months in this type of affair. Joint marriage counseling can't begin in earnest until the Lonely Woman's affair is over.

The First Step: Honesty

Honesty had to return to Linda and Steve's marriage, so I told Linda that she must tell Steve about the affair and tell him that she is seeking counseling for herself. This likely would cause greater confusion and frustration in her marriage, but it would help her feel better and live with greater confidence.

First, Linda told Joe that she was going to tell her husband about the affair. Joe was supportive but asked her to be careful because Steve might get out of control. Although Joe had often said he's supportive of her marriage, he also said he's hoping with all his heart that Linda will leave Steve. This is one of many lies the Lonely Woman believes while in an affair.

Two nights after her first counseling appointment, Linda told Steve about the affair. Steve immediately wanted to know who the other man was and insisted that she leave him. Linda told Steve how vulnerable she had been to having an affair because of her dissatisfaction with her marriage. She also said she truly loved this other man.

Steve then asked if she had slept with this man, and she said no. It's usually hard for a woman to be honest about this right away. Linda reacted defensively and told Steve, "Sex is all you ever cared about anyway." Steve then said he was going for a drive and would be back in awhile. Linda asked when he would be back, and Steve said, "Why do you care? Why don't you just call your lover?"

The Wake-Up Call

Linda's infidelity was a huge wake-up call for Steve, as it is for most Controllers. His insecurity, which was masked for years by his controlling nature, came out in the open. He unraveled fast and told Linda that he would do anything to save their marriage. For the first time, Steve began to look deep inside himself. It's at this point that Steve wanted to enter joint counseling with Linda, but it's more important that he enter individual counseling so he can understand how his controlling behavior has led to his current situation.

Many Controllers, like Steve, must mature as husbands if they expect to succeed in marriage. They have developed patterns of dominating other people and not thinking how their actions and words affect the people they love. Controllers must understand they likely were never taught the skills of how to show love in marriage but that these skills can be learned. Steve must also learn to love Linda in a way that she wants, not in the way he wants or in the way that he thinks she wants to be loved.

The quicker Linda ends her affair, the better chance she and Steve will have to save their marriage. But it's crucial for Steve to let her end the affair on her terms. This is hard for a Controller, but if he demands that Linda end the affair immediately or face divorce, Linda will choose divorce. Instead, Steve should allow Linda time to finish the affair. If she's still seeing Joe after several months, and Steve has worked to change, then Steve should insist on a decision from Linda.

Healing a Lonely Woman's broken marriage is a slow process, and Steve must be patient. The speed of restoration sometimes hinges on how the affair ends. If Linda ends the affair herself, it will help her become more caring for her husband and help build her self-confidence. If Joe is the one who ends the affair, Linda may struggle more with the healing process.

COUNSELING LINDA

Can She End the Affair?

It's very difficult for a Lonely Woman like Linda to end an affair. It may take months of agonizing over the issue, and she may not do it until divorce proceedings actually begin. But ending the affair is the most important part of the healing process. If the Lonely Woman can't end the affair, then she can't understand herself and the changes she needs to make.

The Lonely Woman's ability to end an affair hinges on her moral fabric. Her heart clearly tells her to stay in the affair, but her head says that such a relationship goes against her values. We are often told in American society today that it is healthy and constructive to follow our feelings. This is sometimes wise counsel. But we shouldn't follow our feelings when our actions are in direct conflict with our core values. Talking to Linda about her morals and values was central to the first three months of her individual counseling.

There are several keys to ending this type of affair. First, Steve must be patient with Linda and learn that he doesn't have to control her and every aspect of their marriage. As long as she is involved with Joe, Linda will likely be blinded to any changes Steve makes in his life. But the changes should be noticeable enough that she has a difficult time actually filing for divorce.

Another key to ending the affair is the company Linda chooses to keep. If she wants to heal herself and reconcile her marriage, it will be critical that she has at least one loving friend who believes in the concept of trying to heal a marriage before considering other options.

For Linda, this special friend was Luanne, an old college roommate whom Linda confided in during and after the affair. Luanne understood Linda's hurt because she knew how Steve had treated her. But she also encouraged Linda to consider the big picture and to think about ending the affair to see if Steve would really choose to change.

The final key is Joe's reaction now that the affair is exposed. A married man who is having an affair will rarely leave his family. In that case, the man will usually end an affair with a Lonely Woman who is chronically indecisive about the situation. But Joe is unmarried, so he's more likely to want to continue the relationship for at least another year or two.

If Linda chooses to end the affair, it will give her strength to take a hard look at herself and start a healing process that will make her open to the concept of marital reconciliation. But if her indecisiveness continues for more than a year, and Joe eventually ends the affair, her self-image will be shattered.

This is what I call "The Principal of Least Interest." What I mean by this is that the person with the least interest in the relationship has all the power. In this particular case, the longer the affair continues, the more Joe's interest in the relationship will dwindle while his power over Linda and the affair itself will grow.

Ending the Affair

Linda had a tough time deciding what to do about the affair. She was very much in love with Joe, and she had fantasized about a life with him and a life separate from her husband. Although she pulled back from Joe on occasion, Linda thought the idea of ending this fresh romance was foolish. But when she understood that her children would be deeply affected by a divorce, she finally decided to end her relationship with Joe and try again with Steve nearly five months after the affair was exposed.

Yes, an amicable divorce can sometimes be healthier for children than having them exposed to an abusive marriage. But if Steve changes his behavior, everybody wins. If his change is real, he will be less of a Controller. He will still have tendencies to control, but if Linda is open, honest, and assertive, her love can grow in the marriage.

While it was good that Linda ended the affair on her terms, she still got hurt. Because she loved Joe and didn't want to hurt him, she took great care telling him what she thought would be devastating news for him. But Joe took her announcement in stride, reminding her that he would support whatever decision she made. He became distant and detached at work. This hurt Linda deeply.

"I was upset because he didn't fight for me," Linda said. "I know I was the one breaking off the affair, but there was still a part of me that wanted him to fight for me. When he didn't, I wondered if he really cared. I wondered if he really meant it when he said he loved me or if he was only saying it for the sex. I told Joe that his uncaring attitude hurt me, but he just said, 'You have to do what you have to do. I guess I wasn't that important to you anyway.' That wasn't true, of course, and his attitude really made me angry."

At this point, Linda believed she had to change her entire lifestyle if she was to be happy. If an affair happens with a co-worker, then the Lonely Woman may eventually have to change jobs due to the stress and pain following the affair. A change in scenery can help. But it's important for Linda to recognize that she shouldn't change her core self—the giving, loving woman who cares about people. She needed to learn how to stand up for her ow feelings, opinions, and values, and she didn't need to leave her husband, children, church, and circle of friends to do this.

After five months of individual counseling, Linda felt better about herself but was distraught over ending the affair. Over the next four months, she learned how to heal herself and her marriage. To do this, she had to learn to "talk her thoughts."

Talking Her Thoughts

How do passive people learn to stand up to the controlling people in their lives? They must begin to say what's on their mind. They must learn to talk their thoughts. It was hard for Linda because she had always been controlled by someone and was never given a chance to think for herself and speak about her own issues.

Linda started talking her thoughts with her friends. It's an easy place to start and was especially so for Linda because her friends were excited about her changes. She also began to tell Steve what was on her mind. Steve encouraged this by asking Linda to tell him what she was thinking. Although this was a struggle for Steve, it helped him understand how his actions affected her positively or negatively.

Talking her thoughts to her friends and husband was easy compared to speaking her mind to her parents. Linda couldn't imagine telling her parents about the affair or about anything else remotely personal. The parents of the Lonely Woman often hear about their daughter's affair from her husband whose pain leads him to share his wife's exploits with her parents, his parents, and close friends. In this case, Steve had not revealed anything about the affair to Linda's parents, and Steve and Linda agreed there was no benefit in telling them at this point.

One of Linda's goals in counseling was to learn how to speak her mind clearly to her mother. This is a process that takes time. Shortly after addressing this issue in counseling, Linda had an opportunity to talk frankly to her mother. Her mother had sharp words with Linda's oldest son, and Linda immediately felt the need to stand up to her mother. Linda didn't have the courage to do so, but her awareness of what she needed to say to her mother was the first step to getting the courage to speak up next time. Also, Linda was able to talk to Steve about the situation, and Steve was able to listen and comfort her but did not tell her what to do or give her advice.

These small victories can provide major breakthroughs for people like Linda. This scene helped Linda understand that her marital problems weren't all Steve's fault. Having a controlling mother and a passive father, plus allowing herself to be controlled, also played parts in her affair.

This type of counseling helped Linda not to feel victimized by her upbringing or her marriage. It didn't immediately take away her feelings of resentment, frustration, and bitterness, but it did help her restructure her thinking.

Linda must work on not allowing her parents to continue to control her life. Linda's parents have controlled her for thirty-six years, so they likely won't understand when she tries to change this. She will need to be more open with her parents, saying things such as: "Thanks for your advice, Mom, but to be honest, I just need you to listen and understand me. I love you, but I'm trying to make decisions more on my own."

Just as it's important not to blame her husband for his controlling tendencies, she will need to remember not to fault her parents for theirs. Instead, she needs to forgive them and to change how she talks to them.

Counseling Steve

Breaking His Pattern of Control

Steve had to learn how to stop controlling the people he loves, including his wife and his children. To do this, he first must understand why he has a need to control people. Part of the problem stems from being unable to develop an intimate relationship with his father who was often distant.

"It seemed like my dad was never at home when I was growing up," Steve said. "He was either working late at the office, traveling for work, or playing golf. I never seemed to have much time, quality or otherwise, with him. I saw him even less, of course, when I moved out of the house."

Steve grew up having only emotionally distant relationships with the people he loved, so how did he know how to love his wife any differently? People who are emotionally distant often are insecure, and insecure people like Steve often try to compensate by controlling their relationships.

During his six months of individual counseling, Steve had to learn to let go of the control if he was to save his marriage. This was extremely difficult for Steve, especially when Linda was refusing to give up the affair. This would make even the most secure person feel insecure. Steve worked hard to detach himself from the situation by spending time with friends and exercising frequently. These emotional and physical releases were crucial for Steve to cope with Linda's seemingly unending affair.

Steve also set out to break the pattern of emotional distance he had inherited. He wanted better relationships with his children, and he didn't want his children to learn the same destructive controlling behaviors he had learned from his father.

First, he shared with the children his shortcomings, and he apologized for not being there emotionally for them as much as he would have liked. He also made a commitment to spend time with them and to love them as they deserved. This was an arduous process for Steve, especially when it came to his oldest child, a thirteen-year-old boy. Steve's relationship with Mark was so difficult that they went to counseling and set boundaries and expectations for their relationship. This relaxed and comforted Mark. Steve also planned to spend time alone with each of his children at least two times a month. It was much easier for Steve to deal with his other two children, Emily, eight, and Tyler, five. They were just happy that their dad was spending more time with them.

Helping Linda Grow

To help Linda grow, Steve must learn how to empower her to make her own decisions. He should draw out her opinions, ideas, and concerns, and then listen intently to her responses. He must stop telling her what to do, how to feel, and how to decide things. He must begin listening to her and making her feel that what she says matters.

Steve also will need to give Linda space during this transition. Sometimes, she will feel boxed in, so he needs to respect her desire to be alone from time to time. He needs to understand how important it is not to focus on sex, but rather on tenderness and on being emotionally intimate with his wife. The lovemaking will return if he does this.

Linda needs to start talking more. When she feels Steve is trying to control her, she needs to confront him; but she must be patient while he tries to break this lifelong pattern. Her understanding and acceptance of him while he's making changes is vital because it will give Steve the confidence and security he needs to continue to grow.

Often the Lonely Woman feels trapped by doing this because she feels her husband will return to his former self. This may be a legitimate fear based on history, but she needs to focus on her own commitment to change. If Steve gives up his desire to grow, then Linda, the family, and the marriage may not survive. So it's crucial for Linda not to feel trapped, but rather always recognize that she has choices. Also, because she has chosen to commit herself to work on the marriage for herself and the family, she needs to focus on really being there for her husband.

If Steve couldn't be patient with Linda, then he could likely lose her for good. The Lonely Woman will likely run to her lover if her husband forces her to make a choice between them. The most important things for Steve to do were to be patient, to detach himself from the affair, to work on healing himself and his relationship with his children, and to keep a support system of people who believe in reconciling marriages.

When the affair ended and Linda began opening up, Steve began reaping benefits, because he had learned how to stop controlling the people he loved and how to detach from, and to cope effectively with, the affair. Steve still had, and always will have, tendencies to control just as Linda will always have tendencies to be passive. There is nothing wrong with having some of these tendencies. They can be used constructively in ways that are healthy. For example, Steve can still be decisive, can still say what is on this mind, and can still be focused. But he has learned to do it in a healthy and uplifting way instead of a destructive and demeaning way. He has learned to temper his control.

COUNSELING THE MARRIAGE

The Need to Forgive

Neither Linda nor Steve could be obsessed with the past. They must forgive each other. It was time to move ahead. This is what we worked on when the couple decided to try joint marriage counseling after six months of individual counseling and after the affair had been ended about a month.

Forgiveness is the key to reconciliation. Linda must forgive Steve for not knowing how to be a husband and for the pain he has caused her over the years. Steve must forgive Linda for her betrayal. Forgiveness frees each of them from their own defensiveness and resentments and allows them to start over together.

For Linda, forgiveness may be a process as she tries to move beyond her affair and refocus on her family. It helps Linda to forgive her husband if he's committed to forgiving her and is working on consistent change in his role as a husband. She also must accept that the affair was wrong. She needs to take responsibility for that instead of believing Steve was the reason she got into the affair in the first place. Although his inability to show her love made her vulnerable to the affair, she still took the steps to cross the line.

When Linda has a hard time forgiving Steve—when she's wondering if she made a mistake by ending the affair with Joe—she must tell herself the truth. What is the truth?

1. The affair was a symptom of marital problems.
2. The affair was a result of her finally following through on a risky endeavor.
3. She is vulnerable to falling in love with many different men.

4. Joe controlled her, too.
5. Steve is the father of her children and is trying to change.
6. She and Steve were happy early in their marriage, and that happiness can be restored.

Linda believes she must protect herself so she is never hurt by Steve or another man again. Linda needs time to heal from the affair and all her past hurt, but she also should allow herself to slowly receive love from Steve as he begins to give it. Steve is starting a renewal process of his own and is gaining a strong capacity to show love, perhaps for the first time in his life. Linda must learn to receive this love if she hopes to repair their marriage.

Intimacy
This area was the most difficult to recapture for Linda and Steve. Linda went through months of withdrawal while Steve's need for intimacy and closeness heightened. After the affair was exposed, and during the nearly five months that Linda stayed in it, she had almost no desire to be intimate with Steve. They made love three times during that period, and after the affair was over, their lovemaking increased as Steve's patterns of control decreased. It's important that the return to lovemaking is not rushed, yet it must happen, even if Linda is not in love with Steve. Steve's ability to listen to Linda is the key to freeing her up to at least being open to intimacy and lovemaking.

Linda and Steve were encouraged to spend more time alone together sharing honestly and doing things they both enjoy. They should spend at least thirty minutes each night sharing in love openly with each other, should go out on a date one night each week, and should reserve two blocks of at least two hours each during the weekend for each other. It's important for them to stick with this plan as regularly as possible. During the first three months of joint counseling, they did this with a fair amount of regularity.

With the exception of Luanne, Linda cut herself off from her friends during the affair. It's very important for her to renew these friendships by reaching out in honesty to loved ones and asking for their support in her healing process. This support system is important to her ending the affair and rebuilding her marriage.

Should Roles Reverse?

Steve and Linda had to realize that they couldn't return to the marriage they once had. There were specific things in the marriage that made Linda vulnerable to an affair, and the couple couldn't allow themselves to fall into those patterns if they expected to forge a new, better marriage.

The five specifics were as follows:

1. Steve controlled too much while Linda was too often passive.
2. They spent little time together doing things they both enjoyed.
3. They didn't communicate with their children about their life as a family.
4. Steve spoke before he thought, and Linda rarely spoke.
5. There was no affection or lovemaking.

Here is what Steve and Linda did during their six months of joint counseling to try to ensure that these five specifics did not return to their marriage:

1. Their roles reversed. Steve would encourage Linda to communicate freely, and Steve would become more passive more often. They struggled with changing their old pattern during the first few months of joint counseling. Steve was learning to talk less and to listen more. But when he did talk, he would still give Linda advice, instead of just sharing his opinion and empowering her to share hers. The pattern finally changed during one of our counseling sessions. I asked Linda about her tendency to shut down during conflict, such as the one she had with her mother. She didn't respond immediately to my question. She was thinking. But Steve immediately rushed in and said, "Linda, you have to learn how to stand up for yourself and talk, whether it's with me or your mother." This wasn't a horrible thing for Steve to say, but you could tell that it hurt Linda. She rolled her eyes and sat in silence. I was then able to help Steve see that his goal

should not be to tell Linda what to do or how to feel, but to
let her opinion or her silence be. After that session, they
rarely struggled with this pattern again.

2. Steve would plan weekly family activities and weekly dates
   with Linda doing things they both enjoyed. This area generally went well because Steve really worked hard at it. They
   struggled only twice in this area during the six months of
   joint counseling, both times because Linda wasn't interested
   in doing anything on those particular nights. This hurt Steve
   and made him feel insecure. I warned him that there would
   be times when Linda would withdraw and want some space.
   I told him he shouldn't get upset about it and should not read
   too much into her mood. If it was a family activity, he and the
   kids should just go without Linda. If it was a date with Linda,
   he should cancel the date and not worry about it. He needed
   to give her time. I told Linda that she generally should go,
   even if she didn't "feel" like it. She had to give the marriage a
   chance to succeed by spending time together with Steve.

3. Steve would initiate family meetings at least twice a month
   for the purpose of just talking together about what was on
   each other's minds and about how things were going.

4. Linda would talk; Steve would listen. As Steve listened, and he
   didn't break in with advice, Linda felt free to share more and to
   learn how to open up more easily. They became quite good at
   this by the end of the first four months of joint counseling.

5. Affection was mutually communicated on a regular basis, and
   lovemaking would be done as they mutually agreed to do so.
   The key here was learning what affection meant to each other.
   Linda needed affirmation and acceptance more than physical
   contact. Steve was the opposite in his need for affection.

Making Progress

During the six months of joint counseling, Linda and Steve
made great strides toward repairing their marriage, and both wanted
to continue working on it. Steve became less controlling, but it
was difficult for him, and he sometimes lapsed into old patterns.
Forgiveness was Linda's biggest hurdle.

It helped both Linda and Steve when Linda accepted a job with a
different company. Linda and Joe talked infrequently following the

affair, but memories and Joe's ability to easily move on with life hurt Linda so much that she found it difficult to work so close to him.

Steve and Linda were fortunate. The affair of the Lonely Woman is such an incredibly painful affair that many couples aren't able to reconcile. At least this couple has made progress and has hope for the future.

Recap

Linda's ability to initiate the end of her affair in a way that gives her a chance to evaluate her marriage is the single most important indicator to whether this marriage can be reconciled.

Here is a review of the other critical areas in the healing process of the Lonely Woman affair:

1. Whom Linda chooses as friends after the affair is exposed.
2. Steve's willingness to take responsibility for his part in making the marriage vulnerable to an affair.
3. Steve's ability to reconstruct himself in order to be more fit for marriage.
4. Steve's openness to being patient with Linda as she ends the affair and heals herself.
5. Linda's energy around building her self-confidence and communicating her thoughts more openly.
6. The couple's ability to forgive each other. The couple's willingness to continue to work on healing their family.

Chapter Three
The Double-Life Man

Many men struggle with intimacy and commitment in marriage. It's a struggle that sometimes leads a man into a double life. One life is at home with his wife and children where he is controlling, emotionally distant, and generally uninvolved. His home life usually mirrors what he saw growing up, at least in terms of how he treats his wife. The other life is at work where he is successful, but he works excessive hours and has a series of brief affairs, or at least, one long-term sexual affair. The Double-Life Man accounts for 40 percent of the infidelity cases I counsel, and most of them come from remarkably similar backgrounds. Phillip is one such Double-Life Man.

PROFILE: LOOKING FOR INTIMACY

Phillip grew up in the Los Angeles area, the oldest of three boys, a good student and athlete. As a teenager, he was popular and dated many girls, occasionally staying with one for several months. His home life appeared good on the surface, but his father was a workaholic who was emotionally absent in Phillip's upbringing.

"My dad would come to some of my football and basketball games," Phillip said. "He was proud that I was a good athlete, and sometimes we spent a lot of time together playing or watching sports. But I never felt like I got to know him very well. We never talked about life much. We never opened up to each other. We mostly talked about sports."

This lack of closeness with his father is key in Phillip's struggle with intimacy in his life, and it's common among Double-Life Men. But his father is not at fault because he was never taught how to intimately interact with his children. He learned to be a father by watching his father, and he's only passing on the tradition. And unless Phillip can change his behavior and learn to be intimate, he'll pass the problem on to his two sons.

Phillip's father was a workaholic, and it's common that the fathers of Double-Life Men have addictive tendencies whether it's extramarital affairs, drinking, gambling, pornography, or work.

Phillip's parents had a distant, chaotic, lonely marriage in which little intimacy was shown. Sex is often infrequent for the parents of Double-Life Men because their fathers have their needs met through extramarital affairs or pornography while their mothers withdraw sexually and place their identity in their children. Phillip's mother was unhappy in her marriage and was overprotective and controlling of her oldest son.

"I felt like my mom was always trying to tell me what to do, and that was frustrating," Phillip said. "She used to tell me that I wasn't like other men, that I was better, and that I shouldn't become like other men. She expected me to be the man my father wasn't."

Double-Life Men are emotionally starved and use sex as a security blanket, but they find it almost impossible to stay committed to any one woman. There are two types of Double-Life Men: extroverted and introverted. The Extroverted Double-Life Man will date frequently and live out his sexual fantasies with one-night stands. The Introverted Double-Life Man doesn't date much and uses frequent masturbation to fulfill his sexual desires. Phillip is an Extroverted Double-Life Man.

"I have fantasized about women since I was a teenager," Phillip said. "I dated a lot in high school and college, and I had my fair share of sex. I had a couple of long-term girlfriends, and even though I cared for them, I'd still pick up other girls at bars and parties and sleep with them."

Phillip met Susan at the start of his senior year at Stanford. At that point, he began to feel the need to settle down, and Susan was the beautiful, passive, down-to-earth kind of woman he had always envisioned marrying. Phillip believed he was ready to commit to one woman, but Susan turned out to be a woman who only carried him through the transition from college into adult married life. He soon returned to his roaming ways. On the outside, Phillip appeared to be a balanced man with everything going for him. But on the inside, he was still an insecure boy who hadn't matured emotionally.

A MARRIAGE IN CRISIS

The Honeymoon Is Over

Phillip and Susan had a good early marriage. They enjoyed being together, had a good and frequent sex life, and eventually had three children. But Phillip's old patterns began to redevelop as he started taking out-of-town business trips as a top salesman for a large computer software company. He had two brief affairs with out-of-town women that he was able to keep secret from Susan. He then took a more dangerous step by having an affair with his secretary, Gina.

As with the other two women he had affairs with, Gina is quite sexual, assertive, career oriented, and impulsive. The only difference is that Gina planned to stay in the relationship for a long time. Phillip didn't expect that when he first had sex with her at her apartment after a late night at the office.

To the outside world, Phillip appeared to have it all at age thirty-five. He and Susan lived in a wealthy neighborhood in the Boston area, they were active in church, their three children attended a prestigious private school, and he was in upper management making $200,000 a year at a well-respected company. But after twelve years of marriage, Phillip was about to have his double life exposed.

His affair with Gina was now two years old, and Phillip planned to end it just as easily as he had the other two. But as Phillip initiated talk about slowing the relationship, Gina said she would make life miserable for him if he ended the affair. He threatened Gina by saying he would make sure she wouldn't advance any further in the company if she exposed the affair, but Gina wasn't fazed.

"I knew she had me cornered," Phillip said. "I figured the only way to save face was to come clean. So, I called Susan while I was on a business trip in California and told her I was coming home early to talk to her about a very important matter. I didn't give her any details. When I got home the next day, I told her about Gina."

TREATMENT

Phillip Must Be Broken

In this type of affair, the Double-Life Man is almost entirely at fault. Susan is a caring, attentive wife and mother and never has caused Phillip to look elsewhere for love or sex. Instead, Phillip has a character problem, and if he and Susan hope to recover their marriage, he must change. He must become less self-centered and accept that while he may be doing well in his life outside his home, he's not doing well as a husband or father. This is difficult for Phillip to accept because he has rarely failed at anything.

Phillip is serious about changing. He takes some important steps almost immediately after telling Susan about his affair with Gina. He ends the affair with Gina, then arranges with Gina's blessing, for her to be transferred to a similar job elsewhere in the company. He takes four weeks of paid vacation to concentrate on counseling.

"Susan was shocked when I told her about the affair," Phillip said. "She had no idea anything was going on. She was so upset that she could hardly talk to me. She finally decided to take the kids and stay with her sister for the weekend.

"I thought a lot about my life during that time. I realized that flirting and sleeping with different women carried a lot more risks as a married man than it did when I was in high school and college. I also realized that I was on the verge of losing everything I had worked for and wanted. A wife. A family. Respect. Even my career was on the line. When Susan came back Sunday night, I apologized again, told her I was wrong, and told her that I really did love her. I said I was determined to change and make our marriage work."

Susan wasn't as sure as Phillip. In fact, she was so shocked by Phillip's confession that she didn't know where to turn next. But she agreed to go to counseling with him.

In counseling, I told Phillip he must take several steps if he hoped to save his marriage.

1. Acknowledge his wrongdoing. Key to a Double-Life Man changing his ways is changing his attitude about his wrongdoing. Often a spiritual awakening is a necessary component in the healing of the Double-Life Man. If he doesn't acknowledge the severity of his problem, and the damage it causes to loved ones and himself, he'll just continue in his ways. So acknowledging his wrongdoing has more to do with changing his attitude about himself, about his values, and about his family living.

In Phillip's case, he had already told Susan about Gina, but he also needed to tell her about the other two affairs and about any details Susan wanted to know. "Why can't I just sweep those two affairs under the rug?" Phillip asked. "They happened years ago. Susan never knew about them and never would have found out about them. Why do I have to hurt her again?" But Phillip must start being completely honest with Susan or there's no hope that she'll ever trust him again. He must also make a verbal commitment to start taking responsibility for his every action and to think about how his actions affect his wife and children.

It became apparent early in the process that Phillip was willing to change and willing to understand the need to be a different person. This helped Susan begin to trust him over time. The Double-Life Man, more often than not, doesn't really see the harm his attitude causes his spouse. He thinks since the affair is over, let's move on and not worry about it; it was just a mistake. But often this pattern of not really seeing the intensity of the problems leaves a huge hole in his healing. The boundary problems with women start over again, and the pattern repeats itself within the next few years. Philip's acknowledgment of his wrongdoing was genuine, and the action steps that he took to make some environmental changes early on were also helpful.

2. Change his environment. Phillip took key steps, even before starting counseling, by ending the affair with Gina and arranging to have her transferred. It was essential that either Phillip or Gina was transferred or left the company. They should have no contact with each other, if possible. He also agreed to take time off from work for counseling and to funnel his addictive energy into changing himself. These changes that Phillip made in his work environment were critical to rebuilding Susan's trust and, more importantly, were helpful in surrounding himself with opportunities to succeed and make better choices in his life. When the Double-Life Man does not have an attitude of remorse or sorrow, these changes in the work environment are not likely to take place. He will be more apt to convince his wife that things will work out and that there is nothing to worry about. He will try to give her the impression that things are better, and even provide some documentation, such as cell-phone records, credit-card charges, whatever is necessary to clear his name. But the Double-Life Man will seek opportunities to continue the affair or start the process with another woman.

So these kinds of structural changes are often signs of compromise that need to happen in the Double-Life Man and are also signs that he is genuine about wanting to heal himself and his defects. So what's needed are some heartfelt changes that get to the core of his morality, values, and spiritual life. The changes need to be radical enough so there is not even an appearance of wrongdoing.

3. Restore his family of origin. Phillip must share what he is learning about himself with his parents and siblings, spending time with each of them alone. If they refuse, he must write each a letter explaining the process. It's critical for Phillip to open up to his father, to forgive him for any lingering resentments, to tell him what he has learned about himself, and to show that he loves him or wants to love him. Phillip's father will hopefully share more about his life. If this father-son relationship can change into one that has some depth to it, it will bring a lot of healing to Phillip. Phillip also must share what he is learning with his mother and show her that he loves her. He needs to talk to her about setting boundaries so she doesn't continue to try to control him. Phillip should also talk to his brothers about their feelings toward him. Phillip doesn't have to be the fall guy for his brothers' problems, but he does have to make amends where needed.

Let's take a look at what steps Phillip actually took with his family of origin to ensure his place in the family structure and build their awareness of this type of familial problem.

PHILLIP AND HIS FATHER

During counseling, Phillip was moved to the point of tears on two different occasions while thinking about actually talking with his father. Anxiety, fear, and a deep sense of humility are all things that the Double-Life Man wrestles with intensely. While contemplating talking openly to his father, Phillip said, "If I do that, he'll just think I'm a jerk and ask me what I'm doing and what is my problem. He'll tell me to get over it and move on. Why would I want to talk to him? I already know what he's going to say." This type of response is common from the Double-Life Man in the counseling process. He truly believes that his father will not care, that he will be short with him, and that he will be detached. Sometimes this does indeed happen, but more often than not, the conversation becomes an open dialogue between father and son that leads to some level of awareness and sometimes to a deep level of healing.

So Phillip agreed that although it was not something he thought was a good idea, he would go ahead and ask his dad out for lunch one day. Their conversation focused on superficial things, such as Phillip's work, their family life, his dad's retirement and what he was doing with his time—common threads of conversation, although brief and emotionally detached. Phillip almost decided not to share with his father what he was feeling but instead opened up toward the end of the meeting. He started by saying, "Dad, one of the reasons I asked you to lunch was to talk about some of the problems I've been having at home." His father immediately retorted, "What did you do? Did you hurt Susan in some way?" His dad's response was one Phillip was used to hearing, as his dad more often than not accused and questioned Phillip's actions. Philip was prepared, and responded, "Yes, Dad, I did. I had an affair. I have talked to Susan about it, and I am getting help for it."

At this point, his dad was quiet and mentioned that he was glad Philip was getting help. Then he surprised Phillip by saying "If there's anything I can do, let me know." It wasn't a deep breakthrough. It wasn't Dad sharing about his own life with Phillip, but it gave Phillip a sense that his father genuinely wanted to care. Phillip took his feelings of openness and vulnerability to another level by saying that one reason he had been more vulnerable to affairs was because he had not developed a strong relationship with his father and the other men in his life.

His father said defensively, "What do you mean? We talk. I know you well. You know me well . . . we've had a great life." Phillip responded, "I'm just saying that once in a while it might be helpful for me to let you know, on a little bit deeper level, what is going on in my life and that I am here to hear about your life, if you want that." His dad responded, "Well, sure, son, anything I can do to help. I just don't want Susan to be hurt or anyone else to be hurt. You gotta work this out." Phillip smiled and thought this is the dad I know. He said, "Dad, we are going to work it out."

At the end of the conversation, Phillip knew that perhaps his father would give their conversation further thought, but more likely he would just file it away and not look at his own life too much. But the important thing about this interaction was that Phillip allowed his father an opportunity to be open and allowed himself to talk to his father in a way that brought him confidence, not insecurity, and gave him a sense of being open at a new level.

Sometimes I have the Double-Life Man talk to his father and mother together if I get the sense that dad is emotionally immature and mom is the one who may hear things more openly. In those cases, it is important for the Double-Life Man just to share in general with his parents about things that have been happening, and again, to share his sorrow about it. He needs to acknowledge that he wants to be closer to each of them and have follow-up time with each one alone so his dad can prepare for that time.

PHILLIP AND HIS MOTHER

It didn't take long for Phillip to talk to his mother. After talking to his dad, he felt a sense of renewal, and since he felt talking with his mother would be much easier, he wanted to get it done.

The time with his mother was also beneficial. She was more transparent and more emotional but very thankful that he had talked to his father about the issues. Phillip's mother understood when he talked about his need to be able to say to her what was on his mind while she listened and tried to understand him rather than tell him what to do. Phillip was kind and loving about this process, which also helped his mother a great deal. Often, the mother of the Double-Life Man struggles with her own lack of self-image because of a fairly lonely marriage, so it is more difficult for her to detach and not continue to parent a child who is now an adult. Phillip's mother was gracious and understood what Phillip needed to say, but often the mother of the Double-Life Man continues her pattern of needing to control from time to time. Throughout Phillip's life, he may need to lovingly remind his mother of what he needs. Again, this helps Phillip continue to stay on task and focus on his own spiritual and emotional growth. Those first three steps occurred during the first three months of counseling.

4. Healing close friendships that may have soured. During one of our sessions in the first three months, Phillip mentioned a friend of his at work who knew of his affair with Gina. Brian had given Phillip unwanted advice that this fling with Gina, however fun and exciting, was also one reason he was struggling with his work. Brian was at a peer level with Phillip, so Phillip wasn't threatened by this vocationally, but he was rather taken aback when Brian brought it up. After Brian offered his advice, Phillip intentionally avoided Brian, and Brian knew it. Because he lacked an emotional attachment to his father while growing up, Phillip was able to detach himself from a friendship when he needed to.

But this was a time in his life when he was able to try something different—to reconcile a friendship that had soured, to reach out and say he had screwed up. I challenged him to confront Brian and to ask for forgiveness for his actions and to restore their friendship. Phillip did so, and Brian was very receptive to understanding Phillip's plight. He accepted Phillip's apology as Phillip shared more of what he was learning about himself through counseling. This helped Brian respect and honor Phillip's friendship more. By this point in the counseling process, Phillip had begun to see the benefits of honesty and integrity in marriage, family of origin relationships, and friendships. He saw that this level of emotional maturity made him feel grounded and at peace. Phillip's kind of personality rarely does anything without passion, and it was exciting to him that he was developing passion in an area of life that was at an emotional level versus a monetary level. He was continuing to work hard, but he was also starting a life of thinking emotionally and spiritually more often.

5. Developing close relationships with other men. The Double-Life Man has a developmental flaw that ends up haunting him: He is unable to develop relationships of depth with other men. It is rare that I find a Double-Life Man who doesn't share deeper parts of himself with another woman versus another man. The cause of this is the lack of attachment with his own father. He develops a deeper, more open relationship with his mother and this carries over into his relationship with girls and then with women. This tends to happen outside the home most of his life. Phillip is no exception to this. His inability to develop deep relationships with other men has haunted him and changed the course of his life up to this point. Whether in high school, in college, or in married life, he tended to share more about his life with a girl or woman versus a male.

One of the key areas I addressed with Phillip was his need to connect on a level with another male or two in order to build honesty, integrity, and accountability into his character and into his actions. Phillip's friend, Brian, is a great example of what could happen in a deeper relationship with a man. It is important at this point in Phillip's life to surround himself with men who believe in marriage, treat their wives well, and will help Phillip take the higher road when he makes choices in his emotional and relational life.

In the beginning of treatment, the Double-Life Man is often open to this idea and will look at his current friends for people he could grow closer to. But actually taking the step to open up about his life with another male and to build accountability with that man ends up being a very difficult step to complete. In Phillip's case, I helped him get involved with a couple of men in the church his family attended. He was able to connect with his pastor who thought of some men in his congregation that could help Phillip maintain a level of honesty and openness.

Phillip developed a friendship with a man from the church named Rick. Rick had been married to Kathy for ten years and had two children. Rick was very involved in the church and tended to live out his faith with his actions, giving high priority to family life and marriage. The pastor thought of Rick because he and Phillip had similar interests in sports and business, and he knew Rick would be a good listener, nonjudgmental, and able to open up to Phillip in a healthy manner.

As Phillip developed this relationship with Rick, I encouraged him to have Susan meet Kathy and for them to develop a relationship, if possible. By the end of the counseling process, Rick and Phillip had developed a significant relationship, while Kathy and Susan were not as close. They were able to make some connections as families, but the family relationships did not evolve into their spending long periods of time together. Most importantly, Phillip had developed a friendship with Rick, which along with his friendship with Brian, helped him grow and mature. The neat part about this process is that it gives people like Phillip a chance to succeed in marriage and to break a pattern that most likely has had a stronghold over several generations.

An issue that often arises is that the Double-Life Man is also interested in maintaining some of the friendships he had prior to the affair. It is important that these friendships are addressed as needed and that any healing or reconciliation that needs to happen takes place. Often, I highly recommend that the Double-Life Man break off friendships with other men who have either encouraged him, or have been with him, during his extramarital encounters. This step may seem rigid or narrow-minded, but it is clear that the Double-Life Man has to set aside the things that have entangled him—the things that have made it easier for him to make choices that hurt him, his marriage, and, eventually, his children.

So one of the most effective ways to heal the Double-Life Man, and to ensure the level of commitment to growth, is to control the company he keeps.

6. Restructuring his vocational life. Phillip made his share of enemies while working his way into upper management. It's important that he make amends where necessary because the workplace is an important environment in his life. He may need to talk to his supervisors about not traveling out of town as often as he had. Phillip and Susan also may have to consider that he change companies to get his life back on track.

7. Improving his self-image. Double-Life Men, like Phillip, need to improve their self-image. To help in doing this, I have developed the "Three-Step Guide to a Healthy Self-Image." Susan also would benefit from using this guide, which is printed in full in Appendix A at the back of this book. Here's an overview of the guide:

    a.   Understand how your self-image was shaped by your past. Look at your years as a child and as an adolescent. What messages did you hear about yourself from your family and friends? What shaped your self-image the most? Family life? Friends? Grades? Dating relationships? Jobs?

    b.   Define your current purpose and meaning in life. Do you have a sense of direction in your life? Do you go through periods of boredom and frustration with your life?

    c.   Set goals in the areas of your life in which you lack direction. Where do you lack direction? In your relationship with God, your spouse, your family? In your career, financial, or social situation?

We revisited and reviewed these steps over the first four months of individual counseling. These are all concrete things that helped Phillip make sure his actions reflected what he valued versus actions based on impulses or on feelings in ways that would cause him to slip back into his old patterns of boundary crossing with women, and eventually, patterns of infidelity. For the Double-Life Man, the development of a healthy self-image is imperative to his healing process.

Even in cases where the Double-Life Man is fully broken, remorseful, and repentant of his actions, the personality traits of agitation, control, and a lack of attachment with his wife sometimes remain, even though he may have a sense of humility about them. It is important that he solidify his self-image so that the areas he values most, such as his relationship with God, his marriage, and his family, are validated through his actions.

This process, along with building relationships with other men, were the two most critical components in Phillip's change in behavior. The issues of resolving at some level, any deep-seated concerns or a healing with his father, were important for bringing a sense of contentment into his life. But the actual behavioral and ongoing changes were solidified through the day-by-day choices he made through involvement with other men and through the building up of his self-image.

8. Healing the marriage and the family. Phillip will continue this process while he's working on the first six areas. He needs to share with Susan what he is learning about himself.

SUSAN MUST CHANGE ALSO

Susan has a Lonely Woman personality. She's easily controlled, giving, caring, loved by most, centers her life around others, and has difficulty making decisions on her own. She has been able to endure Phillip's double life because she's passive, dependent, and loyal. While she is in no way at fault in Phillip's affairs, she still must make changes in her life if she is to grow as an individual, forgive Phillip, and heal their marriage.

After learning about the affairs, Susan went into a depression. Instead of seeing Phillip's infidelity as a lifetime pattern that he needed to fix, she put the blame on herself.

"Once he told me about Gina," Susan said, "I asked myself, 'What did he see in her? What did I do wrong? Don't I have what it takes?' I couldn't stop thinking about the affairs. I wondered how often they had sex, where they had sex. I wondered what other people thought of me knowing that my husband was cheating on me. Thoughts of the affair consumed my life."

During the first four months of counseling with Phillip, I also saw Susan individually on a regular basis to help her heal her resentments and work on some specific aspects of her personality that she hoped to change. It was too much to ask Susan to stop thinking about the affairs. Instead, over the course of counseling, I suggested that she think about these statements:

1. It's not my fault. The issues are Phillip's, and he needs to resolve them.
2. I can make choices. I am not trapped in my life. I can choose to divorce, I can choose to separate, or I can choose to stay together.
3. Infidelity blinds a person from the truth. I'm sure Phillip lied to me consistently while he was in this affair. Infidelity and lying go together.
4. The more I think about it, the worse I feel. I can't afford to do this very often.
5. I will take control of my thoughts and decide how I'm going to process my thinking.
6. My boundaries are set. If I choose to commit to the marriage, I know I can't go back to what we had. The double life must end.
7. I know that the double life is a symptom of a deeper emotional problem with my husband. He can choose to figure it out or not.
8. I am very angry with my husband. I've been hurt deeply. But I must choose forgiveness if I am to heal. If I continue to harbor resentment, I will become an angry person and lose the ability to love anyone.
9. I must set goals for myself and my family during this time of healing and choose to let my husband figure out what his problem is.
10. I need to reach out to my friends, and let them give to me during this time. I need them to make me accountable so that I don't stay angry, and, so that I can, over time, forgive my husband, regardless of whether my marriage continues or not.

Referring to these ten thoughts was critical in helping Susan refocus her energy on understanding herself, spending time with her children, spending time with friends that loved her, and continuing to forgive and heal with her husband. Susan's ability to go about this process day by day helped her heal significantly throughout the first four to six months of the counseling process.

I encouraged Susan to take time each week with Phillip to discuss what she's struggling with most. This is not to be a time for blame. Phillip's role is to listen, absorb, express remorse, give reassurance, and offer commitment to change. Susan and Phillip should also spend time together discussing what steps he's taking to become fit for marriage, what changes he already has made, and what he's learning about himself in counseling. Susan must be patient with herself during the healing process and remain committed to overcoming the problems instead of hanging on to her resentment.

It is vital for Susan to take time for herself to build up her self-image. She will also benefit from the Three-Step Guide to a Healthy Self-Image in order to clarify who she is, where she is going, and what her priorities are. This will help her focus on potential hope and renewal and take her away from her obsessive thinking about the affair. As she gains a healthy self-image and builds up security in who she is, this will help her to heal from the resentment and bitterness and move toward forgiveness.

Susan also needs to be open and honest about her feelings as she experiences them. An important part of her growth emotionally will be her ability to not be controlled by her husband's mood or disposition, but rather for her to respond openly and to be in control of what she's going to think, say, and do next. Her openness also helps the Double-Life Man understand her more, meet her needs, and build accountability into his life with her and the children for the first time.

COUNSELING THE MARRIAGE

Phillip and Susan can't recover their marriage unless they both make a commitment to work on it. Phillip began this right away, reassuring Susan his affair with Gina was over. The Double-Life Man must provide evidence of this in a way that pleases his wife. In this case, Phillip gave Susan a schedule of where he would be, and he called her several times a day to let her know where he was and who he was with. Susan committed to working on the marriage after understanding that she couldn't go back to what she had before.

Susan's commitment to this process began nearly six months after the ongoing individual counseling. Throughout the first six months, I would occasionally meet with Phillip and Susan together to review what each person was working on and to help them understand the pattern they were going through. The process of the actual counseling of the marriage did not begin in earnest until six months after the individual counseling started.

Next, the couple needed to develop an environment where honesty could rule. Phillip's double life led to a series of lies. Phillip and Susan must be open and honest about everything, including what they're thinking. This was difficult at first because of Susan's resentment and Phillip's impatience that change wasn't happening fast enough. It was important that they create an environment of honesty so they could openly express both positive and negative emotions charmingly and so they could confess and acknowledge to each other their own personal shortcomings that sometimes blocked them from caring.

They must continue to share with each other what they are learning about themselves, and they must do it in a loving, honest manner. Blame, hatred, and an accusatory style of communication must be eliminated. Revealing information to each other in love helps each person rebuild trust and hope. There were times when Susan struggled to believe anything Phillip said, even though Phillip's changes appeared genuine. This frustrated Phillip, but he had to be patient, understanding, and completely aware of how difficult this process was for Susan. Over time, however, this pattern of sharing openly became a tradition for Phillip and Susan.

It was important for Phillip and Susan to begin spending time together again, just as they did early in their marriage.

They scheduled a brief period of time each day to be together, plus a night out by themselves once a week, and a few hours alone together during the weekends. They also developed family traditions with their children. They had Saturday breakfasts at a bagel shop, and on Sundays they went to brunch after going to church as a family. Spending time with friends also became vital to their healing. Phillip began to spend more time with men who held him accountable for his changes and less time with men who might encourage him to return to his old ways. Susan regularly met with friends who helped her grow emotionally and heal her resentments.

Susan's sexual desire fluctuated dramatically after learning about the affairs. For the first few days she had sex with Phillip to prove that she was still attractive and that she could still please him. But then she became resentful of sex and wanted nothing to do with it for months. It's important for Susan to express herself sexually to Phillip when she wants to, but also to discern whether she is doing it to feel better about herself, or because she feels like making love with her husband. It's OK to do either, but Susan needs to return to physical intimacy with caution, honesty, and tenderness. Phillip had to learn to be sensitive to Susan's need, or lack of need, for intimacy. He learned how to listen and understand fluctuations in her desire for lovemaking and affection. It was common that before, during, and after lovemaking, Susan wondered whether Phillip was fantasizing about Gina or the other women he had had affairs with. Susan often shared these feelings with Phillip, and he reassured her that he was thinking only of her and her needs. Eventually, Susan's thoughts about Phillip and Gina during lovemaking went away.

Phillip continued to spend time with Rick and Brian, who held him accountable for his changes, and to spend less time with men who might encourage him to return to his old ways. Susan regularly met with friends who helped her grow emotionally and heal her resentments. Phillip and Susan healed their marriage after eighteen months of counseling. They're living a renewed and happier life with their children. Phillip decided to stay with the software company, but he travels less. When he does travel, Susan frequently goes with him.

Despite all his changes, Susan occasionally fears that Phillip may return to his double life. It has been critical at these times that Phillip be patient and understanding, listen to Susan, and give her space. He needs to do whatever he can to reassure her of his commitment and love for her.

Recap

Here is a review of the critical areas in the healing process of The Double-Life Man affair:

1. Phillip's willingness to be broken, feel remorseful, and incorporate his faith and values into his daily life.
2. Phillip maintaining lasting friendships with a few men who are loving and good family people. These men will hold him accountable for personal healing and growth.
3. Phillip providing Susan with reassurance of his commitment to their marriage.
4. Susan forgiving Phillip and not holding any significant resentments against him.
5. Susan acknowledging the changes she needs to make in herself in order to break out of her passivity.
6. The couple maintaining friendships with other couples who value the same things in life as they do.
7. The couple creating family time and lasting traditions.
8. Phillip restructuring his time in order to be alone with Susan and each of his children.

Chapter Four
The Passive Man

〇㎜〇

M ost of the couples I counseled early in my career consisted of a Passive Woman and a Controlling Man. But in recent years, I have seen a marked increase in the number of Passive Man-Controlling Woman couples. This type of couple has always existed in roughly equal numbers to the Passive Woman-Controlling Man couple. But they rarely seek therapy because the Controlling Woman is usually content during the child-rearing years due to the Passive Man's ability to nurture their children. The Passive Man tends to be frustrated and unhappy in his marriage, but men rarely initiate counseling. Now, about 15 percent of the infidelity cases I counsel involve a Passive Man. He usually engages in an affair with an assertive, controlling woman who is much like his wife.

PROFILE: A GIRL'S BEST FRIEND

Andrew had a calm childhood growing up in St. Paul with an older brother and sister and a younger brother. He listened closely to his domineering mother and rarely challenged her. He had a distant and nonconfrontational relationship with his father who was passive.

Andrew was nervous and shy around girls and didn't date much as a teenager. But he still had many friendships with girls because he listened to their troubles, and he was safe to be with. Andrew was frustrated by this, but he settled for the nice-guy approach because he had such difficulty being assertive.

In his senior year at Augsburg College, he was pursued by a woman named Gloria. They became romantically involved, and Andrew had his first sexual experience with her. But Gloria broke up with him after only a few months.

"I was crushed," Andrew said. "She was my first real girlfriend. I couldn't understand why she wanted to end it, especially when it seemed like she cared so much. When I pushed her for a reason, she said she just got bored with the relationship. She said I didn't talk enough, and I was more concerned with school and work than with her. She also said—and this one really hurt—that we weren't sexually compatible."

Andrew graduated and went to work for a Minneapolis broker-age firm where he met a man who would introduce him to his future wife, Cynthia. Just like he was with his mother and all the other women in his life, Andrew immediately became the listener in his relationship with Cynthia.

"Maybe Gloria didn't like that about me, but Cynthia did," Andrew said. "We were also a good match in that she never dated much either. She liked that I was helpful and attended to her needs. She didn't get that from whatever other boyfriends she had had."

Andrew and Cynthia married eighteen months after meeting. Over the next seventeen years, they had two boys, and Andrew was steadily promoted at the brokerage firm until he was named a branch manager. While Andrew wasn't a typical aggressive manager, he had good people skills and was well liked by his co-workers. Everything was great at work, but his life at home was suffering.

A MARRIAGE IN CRISIS

Andrew Tires of the Criticism

Andrew loved his boys, now fourteen and sixteen, as nothing else in his life. He spent most of his free time with them and enjoyed taking them to their evening and weekend activities.

But in his relationship with Cynthia, Andrew was becoming more and more like his father. He quickly shut down when Cynthia became angry or when they had a fight. They eventually talked through their disagreements, but Cynthia would have to force Andrew to open up.

Andrew enjoyed it when he and Cynthia spent time with other couples because he was a great listener and friend. This was his true self. But Cynthia often criticized him for giving other people more attention than he gave her. Andrew would defend himself by explaining that he loved her, but it was important for him to help others, too.

"Cynthia's criticism reminds me of my mother," Andrew said. "Both my mother and my wife always seem frustrated about something I'm doing, even if I'm doing something good for someone else. I feel like I can never do anything right in Cynthia's eyes. It's getting to the point where I dread the time I spend with her and look forward to the times I'm away from her, such as at work, golfing with the guys, or taking the boys to a ballgame."

Andrew, now forty-five, couldn't imagine divorcing Cynthia and taking the chance of losing contact with his boys, so he resigned himself to an unfulfilling marriage.

Andrew Meets Rebecca

Andrew hired Rebecca, a single thirty-year-old woman, as a securities representative. He was immediately attracted to her slim, athletic build, beauty, and self-confidence, but she was one of fifty employees, and Andrew had little direct contact with her.

After a year on the job, Rebecca started exercising over lunch at a local health club where Andrew was a long-time member. A friendship soon formed as they began seeing each other at the club more often. Although they didn't work out together—Andrew played racquetball, and Rebecca attended aerobics classes—they began going to the club together so they could hold each other accountable for working out at least twice a week. Their talks during the trips between the gym and the office focused entirely on work. Rebecca carried the conversations well, and Andrew continued his pattern of being an effective listener with women.

Andrew felt great about himself when he was with Rebecca because she was so sexy and attractive. Rebecca was impressed that Andrew was a caring and successful businessman, a combination she thought was rare.

Over the next six months, their conversations turned to their personal lives. That's usually okay if the talk is about what they and their family members are doing. But they crossed into dangerous territory when Andrew started talking about his feelings for his wife, and Rebecca described intimate details of her relationships.

As Rebecca discussed her recent break-up with a man she had dated for three years, Andrew had the perfect opportunity to show his best attributes as he caringly listened to her talk about her pain. This also gave Andrew the opportunity to talk about his discouragement with his marriage and about his love for his sons. This made him look even more vulnerable to Rebecca who didn't mind the thought of crossing the line emotionally with the big shot at the office. Rebecca could also tell that Andrew was attracted to her, which gave her the self-confidence she was looking for following her break-up.

Andrew began to find more and more reasons to cross Rebecca's path at work. He fought back his sexual desires because he feared she might not feel the same way. He also feared that an affair would ruin his relationship with his sons.

Rebecca had developed a physical attraction for Andrew as well. She could tell Andrew was interested, but because he was shy, she knew she would have to make the move if anything was to develop.

Rebecca's Play

Rebecca sought an opportunity to pursue Andrew sexually in a way that would be difficult for him to resist. She believed she would finally have that opportunity when she invited him and other co-workers to an open house at a townhome she had bought recently.

Rebecca scheduled the open house for a Thursday evening, from six to eight. She knew Andrew was going to another branch office that day and would be arriving close to eight, if she could get him to come at all. She knew enough about Andrew's home life to know that if he did show, he would be alone. His boys had after-school sports activities that evening, and Cynthia would have to take them because Andrew would be at the branch office.

"I agreed to go to the open house when Rebecca said it would mean a lot to her if I could stop by, even for just a few minutes," Andrew said. "She had been talking about her new place for a couple of months and really wanted to show it off. Yes, I was aware what could happen between us that evening if the circumstances were right. This was the first time in the eighteen months we had known each other that we would be in a situation outside of work or the gym."

Andrew told Cynthia the morning of the open house that he would be at be at the branch office until about seven o'clock, then he would drop by Rebecca's new place for a short time and would be home around nine. As he always did, he gave Cynthia the telephone numbers for the branch office and Rebecca's townhouse.

"All I could think about Thursday was the open house," Andrew said. "I was nervous, but I was hopeful I could get some time alone with Rebecca. I fantasized about what could happen."

Andrew arrived at her townhouse at 7:45. He sprayed cologne on himself and carried flowers as a housewarming gift. Rebecca greeted him at the door with a warm hug and whispered in his ear that she would give him a private tour when the few remaining co-workers left. She gave him a wink and thanked him for the flowers. The four remaining people stayed a few more minutes to see how Andrew's day went at the branch office. As they left, Andrew said he would stay a bit longer to get a tour. It was 7:55, and Rebecca knew she had some time for her play on Andrew.

Rebecca took immediate control of the situation and asked Andrew if he was ready for the grand tour. Andrew nervously said he was, and they proceeded throughout the two-story townhouse with superficial conversation about how the place looked. Andrew was nervous because he knew his time was short and he had become so enticed by Rebecca that he felt he had to tell her something. Rebecca intentionally saved her bedroom for last. Andrew grew even more apprehensive. He was just about to say that he would like to talk to her about their relationship when she excused herself and went into the bathroom. She returned wearing a skimpy, seductive negligee, gave Andrew a long, full kiss, and began to undress him. Andrew knew he had fallen into the biggest trap of his life, but he wouldn't resist. He felt renewed confidence and satisfaction as he drove home after his incredible sexual encounter with Rebecca. Meanwhile, Rebecca knew the relationship was now hers to control and enjoy.

Where Does Andrew Go from Here?

Andrew and Rebecca continued to spend time together at the club, at her townhouse for lunch and sex, and at an occasional after-work get-together. Andrew also contemplated how miserable he was in his marriage. Cynthia continued to be so controlling and demanding that he considered divorce just to get away from her and so he could invest more energy into his relationship with Rebecca. He thought his boys could handle the divorce because they were getting older, but he still couldn't imagine the thought of letting them down. He also couldn't imagine living without Rebecca.

Cynthia began to feel Andrew withdraw from her emotionally and sexually. He seemed distant more often and refused to talk openly about his feelings. When she would ask what was wrong, Andrew would just say he was tired and work was stressful. This got Cynthia's attention. She knew him better than anyone, and this was not like Andrew.

One day she thought she would surprise Andrew for lunch at his office. When she arrived, his secretary said he was at the club working out. She decided to go there to surprise him, but she was the one surprised when she saw Andrew in a hallway talking face-to-face with a woman she didn't recognize. It was Rebecca. Cynthia's surprise turned to shock when Andrew patted Rebecca on her behind. Cynthia quickly left the club without Andrew seeing her.

That night, Cynthia asked Andrew if he ever went to the gym with anyone. When he said he didn't, Cynthia erupted with anger. She told Andrew what she saw at the gym and she wanted an explanation. Andrew stumbled over his words, as he often did when Cynthia questioned him, and said Rebecca was just a friend from the office and there was nothing to worry about. He admitted he shouldn't have touched this woman and was surprised that he had. He said he was sorry and asked for Cynthia's forgiveness. Cynthia was too upset to forgive him and had trouble believing him anyway.

The next day Andrew told Rebecca what Cynthia saw. Rebecca encouraged Andrew to relax, to think about how wonderful their relationship had become, and to realize that Cynthia had to find out sometime. Rebecca agreed to continue to keep the relationship secret, and Andrew assured Rebecca that she was the one he really wanted and that Cynthia meant nothing to him anymore. But he just didn't know how to leave Cynthia, and the thought of leaving the boys haunted him. Rebecca had begun to grow tired of Andrew's passivity and his inability to stand up for their relationship.

Meanwhile, Cynthia remained suspicious. Andrew was still distant at home, sex between them was virtually nonexistent, and he seemed on edge most of the time. Cynthia spent several hours over the next couple of weeks spying on him and Rebecca at the club. Finally, Cynthia confronted Andrew about the affair, and he confessed.

"I couldn't keep it secret any longer," Andrew said. "I had to get rid of all the pressure. There was so much stress in lying and keeping the relationship secret."

TREATMENT

The Confrontation

Andrew reluctantly agreed to counseling, but had little energy or desire to work on his marriage. Before joint counseling began, Andrew attended two therapy sessions centering on ending the affair and not blaming his wife. This was difficult for him, because he still had a lot of love for Rebecca, and he blamed Cynthia's anger and constant criticism for making him vulnerable to an affair. Although Cynthia's actions certainly played a part in the affair, Andrew's flawed character and inability to be open and honest with his feelings toward his wife were also to blame.

Andrew understood Rebecca was controlling him, just like he was controlled by his wife and mother, but he still found it difficult to end the affair. This is typical for Passive Men who are indecisive in intimate relationships. Andrew found it difficult to pursue Rebecca. Then he found it equally difficult to leave her.

Andrew needs to take the following steps to end the affair:

1. Recognize that Cynthia is willing to work on the marriage and herself. Healing the marriage will help the children feel more secure as they witness and experience their parents' growth and forgiveness.
2. As he confronts Rebecca to tell her he has chosen to work on his marriage, he must remember that healing the marriage will be better than divorce for everyone in his family.
3. When Rebecca tries to talk him out of ending the affair, he must remember that she pursued him. If she really loves him, she will honor his request to end the affair.
4. He must not focus on his feelings for Rebecca. Instead, Andrew must focus on his marriage vows, his commitment to his family, and his new commitment to self-awareness and growth.
5. Andrew must remember that the affair damaged him. Rebecca is not his soul mate. She is his lover. Andrew must realize that he made a mistake.
6. After confronting Rebecca, Andrew must change his lifestyle, including changing exercise clubs. He must have as little contact with Rebecca as possible, which might require changes in his work structure.
7. He must spend time alone reflecting on his childhood, marriage, and the affair. He should think about the changes he wants to make in himself so he can have a better marriage.

Andrew was able to leave the affair because he worked hard on all seven steps and because both Cynthia and Rebecca did their share to help.

Rebecca didn't fight much when he confronted her about ending the affair. She had grown tired of his insecurities and was generally losing interest in the relationship. This isn't always the case for the Passive Man. Sometimes Passive Men go back and forth between the marriage and the affair for months. Their indecisiveness is usually based on how controlling the Other Woman is and how much the Passive Man is working on changing himself.

Cynthia did her part by working to change herself and by patiently allowing Andrew to control when and how he ended the affair. Some Controlling Women, however, demand that their husbands immediately end their affairs. Such an ultimatum almost always leads to a separation or a divorce. Sometimes a separation or filing for a divorce is necessary to force the Passive Man to make a decision about the marriage.

Counseling Cynthia: Taming the Tongue

If Andrew and Cynthia are to heal their marriage, it's important for Cynthia make changes in her personality to make herself a better marriage partner. She needs to stop controlling and dominating Andrew, and she needs to understand that she tries to control him because he is passive and often unable to make decisions about their marriage.

It's critical for Cynthia to work on how she communicates her anger in the marriage and how she handles conflict in general. Cynthia has an expressive personality and tends to have difficulty communicating her anger to Andrew. She often controls the conversation, attacks in anger, and is unable to tame her tongue. This shuts Andrew down and causes him to despair. Cynthia is encouraged to eliminate her temper tantrums and to talk in a nonblaming, open, and honest fashion.

Cynthia was open to changing, especially in light of the affair and the thought of living without her husband.

Let Andrew Make Decisions

Once the affair ended, it became crucial for Cynthia to allow Andrew to assume some decision-making responsibility in their marriage. Here is the step-by-step approach they must take to restore their marriage:

1. Each must stop doing what hurts the other most. Andrew is most hurt by Cynthia's judgmental spirit and anger, so

Cynthia needs to control how she talks to Andrew. She can't tell him what to do or say, and she can't criticize him for what he does or says. Instead, she needs to be affirming and a good listener for him. Cynthia is most hurt by Andrew's lack of honesty and openness regarding anything that is on his mind. Andrew must talk to Cynthia about his thoughts, and he must initiate more time together with her.

2. Andrew and Cynthia must learn to communicate openly with each other about what they've learned about themselves through the affair and through the healing. Both need to be accountable about how they listen and speak to each other. They must be patient with each other.

3. They must restore intimacy to their marriage. Both need to discuss what they desire most from each other in the areas of affection and lovemaking. It is important for Andrew to focus on Cynthia's desire for touching and being close. After the affair, Andrew was still open to having sex, but his need wasn't as great as Cynthia's.

4. They must spend time weekly doing things they both enjoy, plus plan at least one family activity per week.

5. They must forgive. Cynthia was able to forgive Andrew over time because her personality allows her to move on from such difficult circumstances. Andrew had more trouble letting go of the resentments he had buried from the past. His ability to forgive Cynthia for making him vulnerable to the affair was critical to healing the marriage.

In the affair of a Passive Man, the man's inability to tell his wife what is on his mind is often the sole reason why his marriage eventually fails. The Passive Man despises conflict and the work it takes to heal his marriage, so he often finds it easier to stay separated, to stay removed from the marriage. Whether his relationship with the Other Woman works out is not always as important as the Passive Man's need to be by himself.

Andrew and Cynthia were able to heal their marriage through fourteen months of joint counseling, mostly because of Cynthia's ability to be patient, and Andrew's ability to draw positively from the nurturing and solid foundation of his childhood. Both people worked hard to have a loving attitude throughout the counseling, which was a sign of their maturity as individuals and as a couple. These actions clearly prevented an inevitable divorce.

Recap

Here is a review of the other critical areas in the healing process of the Passive Man affair:

1. Andrew willingly ended the affair quickly. The longer he had waited, the greater chance that he would not have been able to recover his feelings for his marriage.
2. Cynthia was patient, and once she learned about the affair, did not act too quickly on her own feelings, such as filing for divorce.
3. Andrew focused on Cynthia's strengths instead of her weaknesses.
4. Andrew stopped comparing his affair to his marriage, and he worked on putting Rebecca out of his mind.
5. Andrew worked hard to not be effected by any conflicts that occurred during the healing process.

Chapter Five
The Consoling Friendship

ⓖⓜⓜⓞ

Most affairs involve a passive person and a controlling person. These affairs usually end or are discovered within a year because the Controller pushes the relationship along. But a small percentage of affairs involve two passive people. I call this the Consoling Friendship. Both passive people in such an affair are indecisive, so neither one pushes the other into decisions about their relationship. This is why the Consoling Friendship can often go on for years without anyone knowing about it.

The Consoling Friendship is a very difficult affair to completely break. The Passive Woman in this affair eventually becomes frustrated because she doesn't want to end the affair or her marriage. The Passive Man also is very indecisive, not knowing which woman in his life to pick. While sex usually is a part of the Consoling Friendship, it is the couple's friendship and their ability to empathize with each other about their miserable marriages that give the affair strength.

The following case is about Emily, a forty-seven-year-old woman who has been in an on-again, off-again affair with Daryl for nearly two decades.

PROFILE: THE CONSOLING FRIENDSHIP

Emily took the role of a Pleaser as a child. She was the middle child of three. Her father, a business owner in a small rural Pennsylvania town, was a workaholic who had a strong will and a

71

caring, giving demeanor. He always had advice for Emily. Her mother raised the three children at home. She noticeably favored Emily's older sister and used Emily and her younger brother as sounding boards for her frustrations.

Emily's identity was shaped by her ability to listen to the advice of her parents. She didn't develop a narrative of her own, and her self-image was based on how her parents and others viewed her to the point that she became vulnerable to being controlled in her relationships. Emily had a lot of close childhood friends.

Moving Out and Moving On

Emily always dreamed of being a nurse. Feeling trapped at home, she eventually chose to attend a college that was three hours away instead of one closer to home.

"I didn't feel like I was my own person at home," Emily said. "I was always having to do something to please somebody else. I never seemed to be able to do anything for myself. I knew I had to go to college somewhere far away if I was going to have my own life and if I was going to get a chance to really be out on my own. My parents didn't really like the idea that I wouldn't be around much, but there was no question that they supported my educational goals."

Emily excelled academically at college and had a wonderful social life that included lots of boyfriends. Although many boys were interested a long-term relationship with Emily, she wasn't serious about any of them, but she remained a good friend to them all. She graduated with honors and took a job as a registered nurse in a town less than forty-five minutes from her parents' home.

While at a wedding reception for one of her college roommates, Emily met Ron, a handsome health insurance salesman who told great stories. Ron was immediately aroused by Emily's slim build and her friendliness. It was clear they were attracted to each other as they danced to soft ballads late into the evening. Fourteen months later, Ron and Emily married. Emily's parents were happy because they were married in her home church and because Ron and Emily lived only twenty minutes from them. Emily, however, was concerned even before their wedding day about her inability to communicate openly with Ron. He was the talker and the dreamer. As usual, Emily was the listener.

A Marriage in Crisis

Emily was overwhelmed after six years of marriage and three children. Ron was financially unstable and moody. He jumped from company to company due to his impatience, poor work relationships, and lack of performance. Emily, who had consistently attended church all her life, became heavily involved in a local congregation. It was a good place for emotional support and friendships. Emily and the children usually attended church without Ron who wasn't interested in religion. This initially shocked Emily, because occasionally Ron would talk about the church he attended while growing up and seemed comfortable getting married in a church.

The Consoling Friendship Begins

Emily met Daryl at church where they served on the same committees and attended an occasional adult retreat together. Daryl, a kind, gentle professor at a nearby university, divorced his wife, Jenny, about two years later.

"Daryl and I have similar personalities, and we became good friends quickly," Emily said. "We became especially close during his divorce from Jenny. I became his confidant. I was sad that he switched churches after the divorce, but it was too hard on him to see Jenny there every Sunday. Even though he left the church, he stayed in contact with me and some other friends."

During the year following Daryl's divorce, Emily spent more time with him and wearied of her rocky marriage with Ron. She was tired of his work and financial instability.

"It was about this time that Daryl and I began to talk about having a life together," Emily said. "I was extremely dissatisfied with my marriage, and I thought a divorce might be better. Even though Daryl and I had a close relationship for three years, we never had sex."

That changed, however, during a church retreat at a remote campsite. Daryl still attended some of the retreats so he could be with Emily and other friends from his old church. On this weekend, Daryl was feeling depressed about his divorce, and Emily was especially angry with Ron. After dinner on Friday, they took a long walk through the woods, talking about their problems. They stopped at a clearing near a river bank, where they held each other for a long time before making love.

"It seemed like such a natural extension of our relationship," Emily said. "We had been such good friends for so long, it just seemed so natural to make love to him. It was all very romantic."

Sex made their commitment to the affair stronger, but their friendship was still central to their relationship. Daryl wished that Emily would leave Ron, but she struggled with guilt about this idea and eventually resigned herself to staying in the marriage. Daryl was disappointed, but he stayed close to her, knowing she would need his support.

Friends Again

Just three months later, Daryl met and quickly fell in love with a woman named Kim. His relationship with Emily faded into an occasional telephone call.

"I was happy for Daryl, but I also wished, more than ever, that I had divorced Ron so that it was me who was with Daryl," Emily said. "But I also believed that a divorce would have been too hard on the children. Besides, Ron was starting to work on our marriage, even though it was about five years too late."

Over the next fifteen years, Emily and Ron continued to struggle through their marriage. During the most difficult times, Emily would turn to Daryl, who was now married to Kim, for support, love, and intimacy.

"It was so natural and relaxing to be with Daryl," Emily said. "It seemed easier to share my problems with Daryl than to confront Ron about our marriage."

Daryl and Emily's passive personalities allowed them to be friends through just about anything, but it also prevented them from deciding what to do with their relationship. Even though there was an innocence to their relationship, it clearly was an affair that served as an escape from their marriages.

During all these years, Ron remained unaware of Emily's ongoing affair because she was consistent at home. She kept the house clean, was a good mother, and still found time to listen to Ron's problems about work. Sex was occasional at best, but Ron didn't mind because he escaped to soft porn magazines and an occasional adult video without Emily's knowledge.

Emily's commitment to her marriage waned more than ever as her children began entering college. She often fantasized about being with Daryl permanently some day. As her children left home, she decided to press Daryl for the first time about making a commitment to each other and ending their marriages.

Regardless of their personalities, women generally want their affairs to last. Even though Emily didn't end her marriage earlier, she didn't want to end her affair, either. This is why she was so hurt when her affair temporarily reverted to a friendship during Daryl's early relationship with Kim.

Emily invited Daryl to their favorite restaurant to confront him. The conversation went as well as Emily could have expected. Daryl felt it was time to end his struggling marriage to Kim. He wanted to wait two years until his only child with Kim graduated from high school, but seeing how focused Emily was on her ultimatum, he agreed to a six-month process of ending his marriage.

The Affair Is Finally Exposed

Daryl's withdrawal from Kim became evident as his sexual relationship with Emily began to heat up again. Kim sensed that Daryl might be having an affair because they hadn't had sex in more than a month. Even when she and Daryl had long fights, they still had sex at least once a week. Kim knew she couldn't confront Daryl about the lack of intimacy because he would probably deny it and then tell his lover that he had to cool it. Instead, Kim investigated the situation herself. She followed her husband for a week, eventually catching him going to a restaurant for dinner when he was supposed to be teaching class.

Kim walked into the restaurant and saw Daryl and Emily at a table together. She began to cry and then impulsively walked to their table and yelled, "I hope you're both happy for ruining two marriages. I'm going to tell Ron right away!" Daryl tried to explain that they were just planning for the next church retreat, but Kim yelled, "Yeah, right! God bless you both!" and left the restaurant.

Daryl and Emily were in shock. They realized they had been found out after nearly twenty years and that Ron would soon know. Maybe the timing was perfect. They were planning to tell their spouses soon anyway, right? Or were they? Emily felt shame and guilt. Daryl felt humiliated and confused.

Once an affair is exposed, it's much more difficult for a man to continue with it and leave his family. This was the case with Daryl. He began to have doubts about leaving Kim.

"The day after the restaurant incident, Daryl called me and said he wanted to get together," Emily said. "It was the first time in twenty years that I was nervous about meeting with him. I feared the worst."

Her fears became reality when Daryl said he didn't want to leave Kim and his son, but he still wanted to call Emily because he still cared deeply for her. Emily was crushed. Daryl was always so indecisive, but this time he sounded different. She sensed that Daryl was distancing himself from her for the first time. Emily left for home in deep despair and confusion. For twenty years, her affair with Daryl was special and fulfilling, but now it was the source of the greatest pain she had ever felt.

TREATMENT

Emily's Confession

Emily told Ron most of the details of the affair before Kim could talk to him. Ron had a breakdown, including a panic attack and some intense shaking. It wasn't an act. He was truly impacted by her revelation.

"He asked what I wanted him to do, and I said I didn't know," Emily said. "I was so confused. I told him I was seeing a counselor, and I thought he should see one, too, but I didn't want to do joint counseling right away. Ron admitted that he had done a horrible job as a father and husband and that counseling might help. Too bad he hadn't figured that out twenty years ago."

Counseling Emily: Healing and Direction

I spent the first two months of individual counseling with Emily helping her to detach from her affair with Daryl. Emily's hurt ran deep because Daryl would not actually leave his family after all these years. She began to question herself, and her own feelings of inadequacy became central in her thinking. She was experiencing significant symptoms of depression and was feeling a sense of hopelessness in her life.

Helping Emily understand she needed to take control of her own life, versus being controlled by situations and other people, was part of her healing. However, this did not mean divorcing her husband and breaking up her family. Often the Pleaser Woman feels she needs to leave her husband because she just can't imagine getting back into that situation.

In the first two months of counseling, two prevailing thoughts raced back and forth in Emily's mind. She would alternately try to convince Daryl to stay in the relationship, then try to tell herself that she never should have gotten involved with him in the first place.

So Emily's healing from the affair was quite difficult. However, she eventually realized that she is an individual who needed to look at specific things in her own life and that her own personality, values, or feelings might need to change.

Emily was encouraged not to blame anyone—Ron, Daryl, or her parents—for the affair. Only she was to blame. Instead, she was asked to look at these issues:

1. She must understand the role as Pleaser that she assumed in her childhood family. She should look at the attributes she acquired during her childhood and decide which ones she wants to keep and which ones she wants to leave behind. She should reveal these things to her parents in love and with the hope of renewal.

Emily was ready to understand these issues in her life. She worked hard at understanding her role as Pleaser and the attributes she acquired in childhood. However, the thought of actually talking to her parents about her life was extremely difficult for her to handle.

In the third month of counseling, we looked at her passivity over the years with her parents and her desire to please them. She often acted as the sounding board for her mother, who in turn, rarely asked Emily about her own life. When Emily shared things about herself with her parents, they rigidly gave advice rather than listening with love. So the concept of actually talking lovingly with her parents about the changes she was working on and what she was learning about her childhood, was frightening to her.

One weekend, when Emily was staying at her parents' home, her mother went shopping, leaving her with the opportunity to speak with her father alone. She opened up to her father about her affair and some of the things she had been learning about herself in counseling. She didn't blame anyone for anything, she just talked to her father about what she was learning. Emily spoke beautifully, telling her father she wasn't looking for advice, she just needed him to listen. Her father cooperated, and their time together went well. Emily was never able to reveal her affair to her mother. Her concern over her mother's probable reaction was too overwhelming. Her father never told her mother about the affair, which demonstrates the level of fear in their family system.

In these situations, when my clients are asked to reveal something to their parents, as with the Lonely Woman in chapter 2 and the Double-Life Man in chapter 3, more often than not, the parents receive the information well but have a difficult time acknowledging their own issues and how they may have affected the child. Again, the important thing is that the child, now an adult who has been involved in an affair, is able to build strength, confidence, and security by talking to his or her parents about the issue. When healing with the past occurs, it is a wonderful experience, and everyone involved grows through it. But sometimes the ties that bind for generations stay bound in spite of opportunities for healing and growth.

2. Emily must ask herself how patterns that were developed in childhood are still a part of her work, marriage, parenting, and affair. What does she like about herself in each of these areas and what would she like to change?

Emily decided that the thing she struggled with most was her inability to talk about herself with other people. During the first few months of counseling, she spent some time looking at different opportunities when she would be able to reveal her thoughts to her friends, to her husband, and to other people she cared about. This experience was very hard and, yet, profoundly important in her spiritual and emotional growth.

3. She should go over the Three-Step Guide to a Healthy Self-Image (see appendix A) and set specific goals in all areas needed.

Emily dealt with the first step in the guide by working through the issues with her parents and understanding her role in childhood friendships. In all of her roles, with friends and with her parents, she viewed herself as the pleaser, the nurturer and the giver. We discovered together in counseling that this role is wonderful, but there has to be a balance with talking about yourself and your needs. Emily was able to start doing that more in her life. Going over these three steps helps the person understand her upbringing, her current purpose in life, and her goals, but each step also has some practical application as she continues through life.

The highlights of this part of the counseling journey for Emily were the following: She was able to talk to her father, she was able to end the affair, and she was able to make a decision to work on reconciling her family. She viewed these as ways she could take control of her life.

I often tell clients that there are three kinds of people in the world: people who make things happen, people who let things happen, and people who ask what happened? Emily was able to start being a person who made things happen in her life that were consistent with her values.

4. She must start with honesty in the home and let Ron in on why she was vulnerable to the affair in the first place.

Emily ending the affair was critical to Ron's ability to look at himself. Ron fell prey to what most spouses of an adulterer do; that is, they have a harder time looking at themselves and working on changes in their own lives until they feel secure that the affair is over. If the affair does not end, but lingers on and on, the spouse may continue to cope with life until the end happens, files for divorce, or ends up involved in another relationship. If we are viewing the affair as the cancer in the marriage, the cancer itself must be treated before the other components of the disease, such as the marriage and the individual personalities, can be healed.

Counseling Ron: A Commitment to Intimacy
Ron struggled in marriage because of his insecurities and his inability to provide nurturing and a meaningful love in the home. Ron was encouraged to stop controlling and to take time to understand the need to love and to provide intimacy and a sense of stability in the home. Up to this point, Emily had provided all the stability at home, and she did it while being in and out of an affair for twenty years.

Ron was asked to focus on his childhood family to try to discover where some of his insecurities took root. As with many controlling men, Ron had a distant relationship with his father, while his mother was a Controller. Ron used humor and sarcasm to mask the insecurities he developed as a child. Ron took his counseling seriously and was able to share with his caring parents that he loved them and was learning some things he thought would enable him to heal his marriage with Emily.

Ron's individual counseling took six months. The helpful part about being a Controller is that generally you're able to be decisive and to move on issues. Ron's ability to do that with his family of origin, and to work daily on the marriage, helped build security in his life. He was using his gifts of decisiveness and risk-taking in ways that actually helped his development rather than masking his insecurities by controlling people.

Ron also learned how to provide intimacy at home. He gave Emily the space she needed to work through her problems. He gave her reassurance of his love for her and the children. He spent time with each of the children individually, confessing his weaknesses, renewing his commitment to love, and offering a closer relationship, if they wished.

During the first few months of counseling, Emily couldn't accept these changes in Ron. She didn't believe the changes were true. She was still dealing with ending her affair and her own insecurities with her family of origin. Ron was finally able to break through the walls of resentment and hurt through consistency, by not pushing Emily, and, most importantly, by learning from two friendships he developed during the process of taking control of his own life. One was a friend to whom he was close in college but had drifted apart from during his married life. Ron trusted Bill and felt he was a person who would always listen and be a good friend. Rekindling his friendship with Bill allowed Ron a way to vent some of his insecurities and problems while he was healing and lovingly reconstruct his thoughts rather than projecting those insecurities onto his wife.

The second friend who helped Ron was a man he had met through his involvement with the city council. Ed had been through a divorce and remarried. Ron told Ed what had happened, and Ed offered to share what he had learned about himself through his divorce. Ed had had an affair, and he told Ron that although he had gone through with the divorce, he had problems in his new marriage, and looking back, felt the affair was not worth it. This helped Ron see that many people are vulnerable to affairs. Ed also shared that after his affair was exposed, his wife was unable to give him what he needed most: patience and understanding. Knowing this helped Ron give Emily what she needed during the first six months of healing. Without his friendship with Ed, Ron's ability to be patient may have been hindered.

How Did the Affair Actually End?

Emily decided that Daryl's decision to stay with Kim after the affair was exposed was the beginning of the end of their relationship. Emily reluctantly decided to initiate a final break-up with Daryl. She was encouraged to tell Daryl by phone, so she wouldn't be tempted to have a final rendezvous with him.

Emily called Daryl at his home. Daryl stayed true to form by being indecisive. He said he would always love Emily, but he just couldn't see himself leaving his family right now. After Emily hung up, she knew she would never talk to Daryl again because of her newfound direction in life. She wasn't in love with Ron—not yet. But the security of her children and her work, and her husband's healing, gave her the confidence she needed to let go of her infidelity forever. Emily's ability to set new goals for herself in family life, work, marriage, exercise, and in friendships was the key to freeing her for a life that had hope and direction.

Another key to healing their marriage was changing their expectations. I helped Ron understand that his expectation for Emily should be that she would commit to reentering the marriage and become a part of the family again. He should accept that her healing process would be slow and that the reason their marriage was better after six months, and they were on the right road, had to do with his feelings and the changes he had made. This helped him feel, not that Emily was never contributing, but, rather, that in her own slow, consistent way, she was there, and she was trying.

I also worked with Emily on her expectations of Ron. She began to understand some of the strengths of his decisiveness, his ability to say what was on his mind, and not always to view this as a negative characteristic. Emily also began to strengthen her ability to share what was on her heart and to be assertive herself. All marriages suffer sometimes from expectations that are too high. We want the best for ourselves, and although this is not a horrific thing to expect in marriage, it can sometimes lead to evaluating our spouse's character, focusing on their weaknesses alone rather than on their strengths.

Congratulations

After six months of individual counseling, Ron and Emily entered joint counseling with the theme of "Congratulations." Their marriage had greatly improved by this time, and both of them needed to feel good about all the hard work they had put into healing their marriage and themselves.

Most of the effort had been made by Ron whose commitment to learning how to provide intimacy and stability in the home was noticed by Emily and the children. Emily's greatest contribution was spending more time with Ron, which helped him believe in himself and gave him hope for family renewal.

Nonblame, nonvictim counseling was critical to their success. Ron and Emily focused on healing themselves and being accountable for their own actions rather than blaming each other and feeling victimized in life. Counseling that centered on self-protection and getting in touch with their anger could have destroyed their hope for healing.

Recap

Here is a review of critical areas in the healing process of the Consoling Friendship Affair:

1. Emily forgave Ron for his years of control.
2. Emily was open to taking advice from friends who believed in marriage and reconciliation.
3. Emily acknowledged her affair and the hurt it caused her husband and others.
4. Ron patiently gave Emily the time she needed to heal.
5. Ron was open to healing some of his own issues and to seeing the role he played in Emily's vulnerability to an affair.
6. Ron became more steadfast and consistent, instead of impulsive and insecure, in his actions with Emily.
7. Emily followed through on the goals she set for herself, her marriage, and her family life.

Chapter Six
The Affair That Never Happens

⟨≀≀≀≀⟩

Can you have an affair if there's no sex involved? Absolutely. I call this the Emotional Affair.

This kind of affair, which may be the most common in America today, seems harmless. Sometimes an Emotional Affair includes people of the opposite sex who are friends and who spend an inordinate amount of time together. Many times, such an affair includes a person who fantasizes about a co-worker or a neighbor.

People in Emotional Affairs believe that because there is no sex, there is no affair. But it is an affair because their lives are consumed by someone who isn't their spouse. They are spending energy on another person that they could be putting into their marriage.

Millions of people are susceptible to this kind of affair at some time in their married lives. It's a subtle type of affair that doesn't have the strength of a sexual affair, but it can be just as damaging.

Emotional Affairs usually occur outside the workplace, often involving married couples with one person from each couple becoming very close to the other. Usually one person in the affair is emotionally healthy enough to stop the affair before it turns sexual.

These affairs sometimes include a Controlling Woman pursuing a Controlling Man. She often is assertive, confident, friendly, and driven; and she usually gets what she wants. Unfortunately, as in the case of Karen, getting what she wants involves an incredible risk to herself and to her loved ones.

Profile: The "Good" Life?

Growing up in southern California, Karen had everything she wanted as a child. She was an attractive, gregarious girl who was popular with both sexes. She was also an excellent student who was talented in music and drama.

She grew up in a wealthy family. Her father was a successful insurance salesman who was able to provide his family with a spacious home in a wealthy Los Angeles suburb, a large swimming pool, a speedboat, a vacation home, a country club membership, and high-priced cars.

"I had a great childhood," Karen said. "I was lucky enough to be born into this wonderful, stable, and wealthy family. I worked hard in school. I worked hard for years learning the piano. I worked hard at acting. But I never had to work hard for money or material things. My parents gave me my own phone line when I was thirteen, my own private studio for piano and acting practice, and my own new car when I graduated from high school. They paid for everything when I went away to UCLA."

Karen was the oldest of three girls, and she was driven to work hard in school by her stay-at-home mother. Most first-born children are driven and hard working, but Karen was also more of a risk taker than the typical first-born.

Karen's relationship with her father was amicable and steady. She developed a fairly deep relationship with him because he took time to talk with her and to support her in her activities and friendships.

Karen had positive relationships with boys in high school. She usually went on group dates where there was little sexual pressure. The summer before her senior year, she met Jeff who attended high school in a nearby city. They both went on to graduate from UCLA, Karen with a degree in education and Jeff with a degree in business; they married shortly afterwards.

"My parents liked Jeff a lot. He always kept them laughing," Karen said. "But they were a little concerned that he came from a lower-income family. They were worried that he might not be able to provide the kind of life they wanted me to have. But I kept reminding them that he was successful in college and that he wanted to be a salesman like my dad. I really felt secure with Jeff, and I trusted him a lot."

A Marriage in Crisis

During their first seven years of marriage, Karen and Jeff had three children and moved to a quiet, middle-class neighborhood where they developed several close friendships. Jeff worked in sales, and Karen stayed at home with the children.

Jeff's income was average for the town they lived in, but Karen was becoming frustrated because she was used to a higher standard of living. She began to realize that Jeff's income was comfortable for now but that it would not allow them to move to a wealthy nearby suburb where their friends were beginning to migrate.

While Karen was becoming envious, Jeff was becoming insecure. He knew he wasn't providing the kind of lifestyle Karen was used to.

Best Friends

Sara and John lived a few doors down from Karen and Jeff. John was a handsome, successful manager in a growing health insurance company, while Sara was a stay-at-home mother of three who was an active member in her community and church.

The two couples became good friends, although they were quite different in many ways. Sara was conservative and reserved, while Karen was spontaneous and talkative. But they became good friends and saw each other almost every day while their kids played together. Jeff was still witty, although his lack of business success was eroding his self-confidence. He was becoming more insecure and uptight. John was impulsive and arrogant. Jeff preferred softball and other team sports, while John liked boating, hiking, and camping.

"They were our best friends in the neighborhood," Karen said. "We would go out as couples at least once a month, and for several years, we took a few days each summer to rent a cabin together at a nearby resort."

They Begin to Cross Boundaries

Karen, now thirty-four, was attracted to John. She loved his confidence, his success, and his ability to relax and enjoy life. He seemed so different from Jeff. She began fantasizing about John, dreaming of being alone with him at the resort they rented in the summer and being romantically pursued by him. The more Karen fantasized about John, and the more she compared and contrasted the two men, the more her feelings for Jeff deteriorated.

Although Karen didn't know it at the time, John was fantasizing about her. He was attracted to her body, her humor, and her confidence.

When the couples got together, Karen and John talked together, and Sara and Jeff did the same. While Karen and John seemed consumed with each other, Sara and Jeff focused on their marriages, not on each other. Sometimes this can be the difference in marriage between Controllers and Passive people. Controllers, like Karen and John, are more likely to quickly cross boundaries regardless of how happy they are in marriage, while Passive people, like Sara and Jeff, take much longer to do so, and usually won't unless they're in a terrible marriage. Controllers are impulsive and take risks. This can be healthy, but Karen's impulsiveness was about to get her into an affair that could severely damage her marriage.

A Near Miss

Karen was beginning to feel the dilemma she was in. She realized she had to decide if she would pursue her best friend's husband.

"Going after John went against everything I believed in and valued," Karen said. "But my feelings for him were becoming so intense, and I was so unhappy with Jeff. It's almost like I couldn't stop myself from acting on my feelings."

On a hot Saturday afternoon in July, Karen was alone for a couple of hours while Jeff took the kids to the city pool. She knew John was working in his yard and that Sara was visiting her parents, but she didn't know if John's children were home. Karen slipped into her shortest jean shorts and a revealing summer top, and impulsively walked over to visit with John. He invited her into the backyard for some iced tea, and he mentioned that the kids were downstairs watching a movie.

They started with some small talk about their families and then began to poke fun at each other's spouses and their insecurities. It was clear both felt they were a cut above their spouses. A mutually-shared belief of having inadequate spouses is one of the biggest danger signs of an impending affair between friends.

John and Karen talked about some of their feelings for each other. As the sense of intimacy and romance built, Sara drove into the driveway. John and Karen withdrew from each other and acted calm as Sara joined them in the backyard. The three of them chatted awhile before John excused himself to go back to trimming hedges. As Karen walked home later that day, she wondered what would have happened if Sara had not come home when she did. And she wondered what would happen next.

A Reality Check

Whether they realized it or not, Karen and John were having an affair at this point. Karen's affection for John was affecting how she viewed Jeff. It's true that people may compare their spouses to others and that they may even fantasize about others from time to time. But if they're involved with another person at an emotional and romantic level that affects their ability to love their spouse, then they're having an affair.

Karen felt trapped. She believed she had outgrown Jeff. She even believed that she may have married the wrong person. John seemed so much more like her. Karen didn't understand, however, that her feelings for John were part of the reason for her frustration with Jeff.

She fantasized about divorcing Jeff and marrying John. She liked the idea of mothering John's children, who knew her so well already. Looking ahead in a way that removes them from the realities of life and into a hopeful view of a new world with the "right" spouse is common for people in an Emotional Affair. It's one thing to fantasize about another person emotionally or sexually, it's another to carry the fantasy into a planned reality. It was clear that Karen's thoughts were centered around John, and not Jeff.

Karen was at a major crossroads in her life. Would she pursue the affair, or would she work on her marriage? Such a choice usually depends on how emotionally healthy the person is. The more unhealthy the person, the more likely he or she will pursue the affair, and it will turn sexual.

Advice from Friends

Karen decided to seek the advice of Meredith, one of her best friends from college with whom she still had lunch occasionally. Meredith had had a good marriage for more than fifteen years and usually demonstrated a great deal of wisdom and discernment about life.

Karen invited Meredith to lunch and immediately began telling her about her frustrations with Jeff. She then talked about John and her confusion about what to do next. Meredith said she understood how exciting it must be to have passion for a man again. Her only advice was that Karen should do whatever she would advise her best friend to do if she was in a similar situation.

"My heart just sank when she said that," Karen said. "That wasn't the recommendation I was looking for at all because I knew that I would advise my best friend to work on her marriage. Deep down, I knew she was right, but I didn't want to accept it."

Karen then decided to talk with Brenda, a divorced woman she knew from church.

"Brenda was divorced, and then she had a difficult break-up with a man she had been dating," Karen said. "So I was sure she would understand what it's like to be frustrated in a marriage."

Brenda told Karen about her need to be free from her ex-husband's control and to start doing things for herself. Brenda had a lot of anger toward her ex-husband and her ex-boyfriend. She said she learned that she shouldn't settle for a mediocre marriage, she deserved the best. That made sense to Karen. It was clear to her that she was settling for Jeff. If she deserved the best, then she should have John.

Nothing changed. Karen still obsessed about John to the point that she was upset that he didn't tell her when he left for a ten-day business trip. At home, she became more and more critical of Jeff and told him that she needed some space.

At one of the children's birthday parties, Karen's mother noticed that she seemed preoccupied and asked her what was wrong. Karen told her she was frustrated with Jeff's insecurities and lack of career advancement and her diminishing respect and love for him, but she said nothing about John. Karen's mother was understanding and encouraged her to see a counselor.

TREATMENT

Counseling Karen: Direction Is Needed

Many of the women I counsel are like Karen: They're frustrated with their marriage and have met another man. But most of those women are already having a sexual affair. Karen had enough control over her emotions to at least get some objective counseling before she continued her affair and risked adultery. If Karen can break her affair at this point, she can make the healing and forgiveness stage of reconciliation easier on herself and her husband.

During the first couple of sessions, Karen looked at how she had gotten to this point. It was obvious that her feelings for John had paralyzed her ability to see any of her husband's positive attributes. She was giving John all her positive energy, making it impossible for her to love Jeff. Karen didn't agree with this perspective because she knew her feelings for Jeff were tarnished before she fell for John.

Karen was encouraged to look at her childhood to see if she had developed patterns early in life that made her susceptible to this affair. Karen succeeded at anything she put her mind to and generally got anything she wanted. This trait hurt her in this case. She wanted John and set aside all other thoughts in order to catch him.

"I understood that I could still have John if I wanted him, but at what cost?" Karen said. "My marriage would be shattered. My children would never be the same. Both our families would be devastated. Was having John worth it? But I also had to think about whether putting energy back into my marriage was worth it. Could I regain the feelings I once had for Jeff?"

Karen was having a hard time letting go of John, and she was convinced that she could never love Jeff again.

Her Heart Is Touched

When Karen got home from her second counseling appointment, she saw a sight that really touched her heart. Jeff was on the back porch swing with their three children—one on his lap and the others on either side of him. They were all content and happy.

"I realized at that moment that it wasn't worth destroying my family just to be with John," Karen said.

Many people refuse to work on their marriage solely for the sake of the children because they say it's unfair that the children grow up in an unhealthy home. But my experience shows that children have a very difficult time coping after a divorce. Having a divorce is a heart attack for the parents and diabetes for the children. The children may not feel as much of the pain as early as the parents do, but they suffer emotionally for the rest of their lives. If the marriage is violent, then the children need protection and a divorce may be preferred. But this was not the case with Karen and Jeff, and it's not the case in most marriages.

Karen decided to end her Emotional Affair with John. She didn't want Jeff to know anything about the affair, but she wanted to talk to John again and let him know her decision. These thoughts are common for the adulterer. She believes the affair should be kept a secret from her spouse, yet her "lover" should know what is happening. Karen actually needs to do just the opposite. Telling Jeff about the affair brings accountability and openness to the situation. Jeff needs to know. It may devastate him, but it will more likely ensure that Karen will stay out of the affair and be committed to healing the marriage. Jeff will cope over time. John doesn't need to know anything. If Karen insists on some communication, she should send him a brief, curt, to-the-point letter that ends the relationship and makes John aware that she's committed to working on her marriage.

It's rare that the woman will end her Emotional Affair this way. She usually sees the man again, and the man encourages her to reconsider. It will be hard for Karen to end the affair, but considering her personality, she should be able to accomplish it, if she just puts her mind to it.

Karen wrote John a letter that was brief and detached. John was surprised by the letter and a bit annoyed by Karen's change of heart. But he respected her wishes, and by doing so, he assured that Sara most likely would never find out about his attraction to Karen. What Karen didn't know until later was that John had already had two brief affairs over the previous four years.

Counseling Jeff: Rebuilding

When Karen told Jeff about her affair, she said she had been struggling with the marriage for years, and she was feeling very unfulfilled. She talked about her frustrations with Jeff and her feelings for John. She said nothing had happened between her and John and that she had ended that relationship and wanted to work on her marriage. Jeff wept quietly, but generally stayed composed and said he would have to think about all that she had said. But he did agree to see her counselor, especially considering that the counselor encouraged Karen to do what was good for her marriage and family, not what felt good at the moment.

Jeff's self-confidence was shaken more than ever after Karen's announcement. He knew he had been insecure and rigid, but he didn't feel that was any reason for Karen to build a relationship with John. He also was angry with John. Jeff was encouraged to express his anger and hurt to Karen, but to remain focused on healing the marriage.

Before Jeff could focus on healing the marriage, he needed some individual sessions to understand where he got off track. As it is with many men, Jeff wrestled with the concepts of being content versus complacent in a marriage. Contentment in marriage means being fulfilled but also having some direction and growing. Complacency has to do with apathy, staying stuck, and not growing.

Jeff's complacency in marriage had to do with the fact that things other than his marriage had become more important in his life.

One of the difficult things for most men to understand about themselves as they enter into marriage is that unless they saw a lot of nurturing, and unless they saw their father freely serving their mother in a loving way, they tend to detach from the marriage and family and become more consumed with the worries of the world. This was clearly the case for Jeff, and part of his rebuilding process was to start showing on a daily basis that his marriage and family were of high value to him. He had a good foundation growing up and that helped him learn some skills more quickly for focusing on family time and marital intimacy.

Within the first two months of our individual time, Jeff was able to understand that his financial insecurities stemmed from the fact the majority of his self-image was in the amount of money he made. Because of his limited income potential, he developed a rigidity toward financial issues, which was really a projection of his own feelings of inadequacy. Our time together dealt more with restructuring his life and his value system and increasing the amount of time he spent with his family versus the amount of time he was fretted over job fears and feelings of financial impairment. This personal reassessment helped him gain more confidence at work, a fresher perspective, and more job success.

Jeff also learned early in the individual counseling process that Karen might not be receptive to all of his changes and that he should be patient with her. There were times when Jeff was frustrated, but again the counseling helped him put his expectations in perspective. This helped him detach from Karen during the times he felt most high and adequate.

Jeff and Karen also began together to pursue friendships that they had let lapse over the past few years. They were able to start spending time as a couple with other couples that they had been close to. Doing this monthly, helped build emotional and spiritual security back into Jeff's life and helped build the family's sense of security as well.

Jeff's individual counseling process lasted three and a half months. As this counseling was winding down, the process of counseling the marriage began.

Counseling the Marriage: Lost Keys

During joint counseling, Karen and Jeff were asked to share what drew them together in the first place. They were able to see that their steadfastness and their acceptance of each other were two of the keys they had lost. They had become more and more critical and unaccepting of each other's shortcomings to the point that that was all either one could see. Their steadfastness had turned into boredom and isolation. They needed to retrieve these two keys by following these principles:

1. Decisions in the marriage must be made mutually. Both Karen and Jeff had developed an attitude of "mine" and "yours" instead of "ours." Jeff needed to become less rigid with finances, and Karen needed to be more accountable in this area. Communicating with a mutual sense of direction would help them rediscover the key to steadfastness in their life together.
2. Focus on each other's strengths. Both were guilty of focusing on each other's faults. This destroyed the foundation of their marriage. Their ability to accept each other through good and bad times used to be one of their greatest strengths as a couple.
3. Revive courtship memories. They were instructed to dig up any old notes and letters they wrote to each other during their courtship and marriage and to read one note or one letter daily for two weeks. The purpose here was to have them remember the things they did for each other that helped them grow together.

Jeff and Karen worked hard at healing their marriage, although Jeff still obsessed occasionally about why Karen pursued John, and Karen continued to think about John from time to time. I helped them understand that this type of thinking brought out their worst and would set back the healing process.

Within four months, Karen and Jeff were well on their way to forgiveness and renewal in their marriage. This happened in such a short period because:

1. The affair stayed at the emotional level and never turned sexual.
2. Karen is a Controller and can eliminate certain emotional feelings quickly if she wants to.
3. Jeff worked hard on rebuilding his confidence and security.
4. Karen gave Jeff the reassurance he needed. She took time to talk to him, and they spent time together alone and as a family.
5. The relationship with John and Sara became distant. Not all Emotional Affairs end this quickly. Many drag on for years, putting a stranglehold on an already flat marriage. The earlier an Emotional Affair can be recognized and dealt with, the greater the likelihood that it will end without doing irreparable damage to the marriage.

Secrecy is the main reason Emotional Affairs carry on into sexual affairs. That's why a few chosen people who love you should know about the relationship as early as possible. They will provide objective advice. The secrecy of the affair is extinguished by others knowing about it.

Emotional Affairs can be prevented if people clearly draw lines in their relationships with the opposite sex. It's important to have both male and female friends, but friends of the opposite sex should be people your spouse knows well. You have only so much energy to give to others. People must save their best for their marriage and family.

Jeff and Karen never told Sara about the affair, although they were encouraged in counseling to do so. Karen remained distant from John with a few exceptions, but she still saw Sara frequently, although on a less regular basis. Jeff and John ended their relationship completely. The children from both families still played together regularly, but they never went on a summer trip together again. Sara and John eventually moved to a wealthy Los Angeles suburb.

Recap

Here is a review of other critical areas in the healing process of the Affair That Never Happens:

1. Karen kept the affair at an emotional level.
2. Karen sought wise counsel from friends.
3. Karen decided to work on healing her family instead of following her feelings.
4. Karen focused on Jeff's strengths instead of what she finds frustrating about him.
5. Jeff forgave Karen and understood her vulnerability to this emotional affair.
6. Jeff's openness to making some changes in his attitude and character in order to enhance his marital life.
7. Jeff became less rigid in his financial control and sought Karen's mutual agreement in this sensitive area.
8. Jeff and Karen's desire to do activities together that both of them enjoyed.

Chapter Seven
The Affair of the Future

⟨◌⟩

There is a new kind of Emotional Affair surfacing in America. I call it the Cyber Affair. Instead of having an Emotional Affair with a neighbor, a co-worker, or a friend's spouse, more and more people are having Emotional Affairs with someone who lives across the country or even on the other side of the world. This, of course, is the result of the Internet and the other technical wonders of the past few years.

While Cyber Affairs are not currently among the top five affairs in America, they very well could be by the end of the century. By then, it's likely most Americans will have access to the Internet and to other on-line chat services through computers at home and at work.

Most people who have Cyber Affairs never meet in person. Many times it's virtually impossible because they live in different parts of the country. It will be interesting to see how Cyber Affairs change as technology improves. It's likely that more and more people will have cameras attached to their computers, allowing people to see whom they're chatting with. Being able to see that person will diminish the strength of the affair quickly if there is no physical attraction for one of the individuals, but it will add a lot of power to the affair if there is a physical attraction. This will lead to more face-to-face meetings, which will lead to more sexual affairs.

The amazing thing about Cyber Affairs is how quickly they become Emotional Affairs through the depth of written conversation. People chatting on the Internet have few qualms about revealing the most personal details about their lives and marriages. Cyber Affairs can easily continue because they're nonthreatening, convenient, and secretive. They sometimes become sexual affairs when the people insist on meeting each other.

Treatment of Cyber Affairs is most successful if the person having the affair is a Passive Woman who keeps the affair at the emotional level. But if it's a Double-Life Man or a Controlling Woman who is having the affair, their addictive personalities make their Cyber Affairs more difficult to treat.

Most of the couples involved in Cyber Affairs include a lonely, introverted, nurturing woman and a controlling, extroverted man who has just learned what his wife has really been doing on the computer all those hours. Typically, the man who the wife is having the affair with is also introverted and either single or divorced. People who are involved are usually in their thirties or forties, such as Anita, a forty-three year-old Ohio woman.

PROFILE: A CHILDHOOD TURNED UPSIDE DOWN

Anita's early years, growing up the oldest of two children in a Cleveland suburb, were positive. She spent most of her time with her mother, who didn't work outside the home, her brother, Amos, and her neighborhood friends. Her father traveled out of town for his sales job and wasn't home much of the time.

But her life became turbulent when her mother and father unamicably divorced when she was fourteen. Anita lived with her mother but became the go-between for her parents as each leaned on her to communicate with the other and to share their frustrations about the other. Her father remarried a year after the divorce and moved to a nearby suburb.

"It was really hard on Amos and me to deal with Dad's new wife," Anita said. "We couldn't understand why he remarried so fast. We were hoping that he and Mom would get back together, so it was a real blow when he remarried. It was also hard living with Mom because the divorce really hurt her. And she really had a hard time dealing with my dad's new wife. She really resented him, and she let us know it. Thank goodness I had a lot of friends I could lean on. I loved getting out of the house to do things with my friends."

After high school, Anita studied education at Ohio State University.

"I really enjoyed my college years," Anita said. "It was so good to be on my own and away from my parents. The only bad part of those years was coming home for holidays and having to spend time with my parents as they built their new lives."

Just before her senior year, Anita married William, a man she met at Ohio State. Like Anita's father, William pursued a career in sales and business management. But within the first year of the marriage, William began drinking heavily and began physically abusing Anita. She went to counseling for six months but it helped little, and she filed for divorce.

Shortly after the divorce, Anita got a job teaching sixth-grade students in Cincinnati. About four years later, Allen transferred to her school to teach sixth grade, and they soon began dating.

"Allen was popular," Anita said. "He was expressive and spontaneous, and he had a fun-loving spirit. He loved to take risks. I was still pretty cautious because of what had happened with William, but Allen was so persistent and charming, and I loved him so much that I finally agreed to marry him. It only took me about four years to come around."

A Marriage in Crisis

The first five years of their marriage were great. Allen and Anita spent a lot of time together, including driving to school and home together. But their marriage began to suffer after the birth of their two sons, Caleb and Jeremy. Allen became distant and worked more. Although he spent time with the boys, Anita felt his disciplinary style was too harsh. They argued more frequently, and their conflicts often weren't resolved lovingly. Allen also became more controlling in the marriage. After nine years in her second marriage, Anita returned to counseling.

"I learned how to stand up for myself in a loving way," Anita said. "I also learned how to get away from Allen emotionally if I wanted to, and I learned how to take more control in my marriage. My counselor helped me understand that I could make choices in the marriage, too. Allen even went to some counseling later on and that helped him change his behavior in some ways."

Allen eventually left teaching and opened his own marketing company. He became consumed with his new endeavor and returned to his old patterns of being distant and controlling. He was gone most weekday evenings. Anita was left frazzled, overworked, lonely, and unfulfilled.

Friends Who Care

While Anita wasn't satisfied with her marriage, she was happy at work. Her job was satisfying, and she developed a network of female friends at the school who were loving and supportive.

"We started going out once a week—you know, a girls' night out," Anita said. "We especially enjoyed poking fun at the men in our lives, including Allen. I know it wasn't very nice of me, but it really helped me get some things off my chest about my marriage."

This group of women had a poor outlook on men. Three of the four had unhealthy relationships with their boyfriends, and two of the boyfriends ended up cheating on them during their dating relationships.

Anita and her friends began talking about a woman's needs for freedom and independence, and they began balking at the idea of monogamy.

"Men have never been monogamous," Anita said. "We figured if they aren't, then we didn't have to be, either."

Cruising the Internet

Anita's family bought a computer when the boys started school. The boys used it to play games and to help with their school work, but everyone enjoyed it. Allen had gotten involved with computer programming in his work, and he liked developing family budgets and surfing the Internet for interesting websites.

Anita also used it. When Allen wasn't home—which was often—and once the boys were in bed, she would often turn to the Internet's chat rooms to relieve some of her loneliness.

One night, she began chatting over the Internet with Hugh, a recently divorced man who said he was sympathetic to the problems Anita was having in her marriage. He also believed that the concept of monogamous relationships was for a time long past.

"Hugh was so charming," Anita. "I know I had never met him, and I hadn't even heard him talk, but he had such a wonderful way with the written word. I felt like he was in my living room listening to and understanding every one of my problems. He really seemed like he understood me."

After that first night, Anita and Hugh agreed to meet in the same chat room the next night at the same time. An Emotional Affair was blossoming. An Emotional Affair on the Internet is different than one that starts with face-to-face meetings. There are almost no boundaries with an Internet Emotional Affair. People quickly cross into intimate conversation and sexual innuendo.

The Internet is a wonderful outlet for people who want to get to know each other, develop relationships, and have stimulating conversations. There are no inhibitions and no issues of physical intimidation, so most feel comfortable as they explore these situations with other people. For single people, there is a lot less confusion than there can be in a bar, a singles group, or some other community gathering. For married people, an Internet chat room can be a private, secret place to live out fantasies and to push the boundaries of infidelity without their spouse ever knowing.

Hugh and Anita's on-line relationship turned romantic over the next two months. Hugh became insistent that he and Anita meet. Anita was initially against the idea because she feared getting caught and was unsure what she was getting herself into. Hugh remained patient, but he continued to push the relationship. Next, he telephoned Anita at a time when he knew Allen would be out of town.

"I was so surprised by his call," Anita said. "I was worried that he wouldn't sound like he wrote, but I wasn't disappointed. We had a great conversation. He asked if I would meet him at a nearby restaurant, and I almost agreed. I really felt secure enough with him to think about it seriously. But I still turned him down."

Allen's on the Line

Hugh and Anita continued to chat over the Internet with an occasional phone conversation sprinkled in. Meanwhile, Anita's belief that she could have close male friends became even stronger.

Hugh continued to push Anita to expand the relationship. His next step was to call her during a time when Allen might be home.

"Allen wasn't home yet, but I was really upset that Hugh would take a chance such as that," Anita said. "I knew Allen could be home at any time, and I became a little paranoid and took the cordless phone into the bathroom to talk to Hugh."

When Allen came home, he heard Anita talking in the bathroom about her romantic feelings for another man. Allen impulsively ran into a bedroom and picked up the phone there. He demanded to know who was on the other line and told Anita to get off the phone. When Anita told Allen to back off, Allen angrily hung up the phone, stormed into the bathroom, grabbed the phone from Anita, and hung it up. Anita began sobbing and told Allen that he was always trying to control her.

"After we both settled down, we had a pretty honest discussion about what was going on," Anita said. "I told him there was nothing going on between Hugh and me but that there wasn't anything wrong with me having a close relationship with another man as long as it didn't turn physical. I told my friends about the incident the next day, and they all supported me. They said they couldn't believe Allen had been so angry. They even said that I should be free to explore other relationships because that would help me grow. They said if Allen disagreed, then he must be insecure and not love me."

Allen did disagree. He felt hurt, angry, violated, and rejected. To spite Anita and to try to teach her a lesson, Allen called a sex line for sexy talk and support. He hoped Anita would be outraged by his phone calls, but instead she told him that he was being immature. Anita said she was developing mature relationships on the Internet. She compared his calls to one-night stands.

Although Allen believed Anita would be hurt if he developed a relationship with another woman, he knew his phone-sex strategy wouldn't work. He then turned to counseling.

TREATMENT

By the time he entered counseling, Allen had left home until Anita made a decision about her actions. Such an abrupt separation has the potential to be quite damaging. The longer the separation lasts, the more difficult the healing will be. Anita didn't want Allen to return right away because his leaving was so impulsive and hurtful. Allen didn't want to return until his wife saw things his way. In the end, however, it was Caleb and Jeremy that were hurt most by these power plays.

Both Anita and Allen must take some blame for this Cyber Affair. Anita's current value system and subsequent actions are certainly a violation of their marriage. But Allen must also examine his controlling behavior and inability to love his wife in a way that brings out her best as a reason why she may have been vulnerable to the affair. Anita must stop chatting with Hugh, and Allen must tell Anita he's hurt by her actions, and he wants to work on their marriage.

Making Allen More Secure

For his part, Allen must become more secure as an individual. There are several steps he must take.

1. **Address the hurt.** First, he must talk with Anita about how hurt he was by her Emotional Affair. He should tell her that he's not interested in controlling their marriage anymore but wants to work on healing their relationship and learning how to bring out her best (see Appendix A).

2. **Improve his self-image.** Allen must examine his life, including his childhood, to understand what patterns he has developed that have resulted in his current personality and outlook on life. Allen learned, for instance, that he became

more controlling when his sons were born. This was because his parents weren't good role models, and he sometimes felt incapable of providing intimacy for his children. Because he was insecure in this area, he became more controlling to compensate. At this point, Allen decided what he wanted to change about himself and set specific personal goals for his life. Controllers like Allen enjoy doing this because the focus is on them as they realize how insecure they become when they feel out of control. Allen also benefited from completing the Three-Step Guide to a Healthy Self-Image.

3. **Share his story with Anita.** After his third counseling session, Allen shared with Anita some of the things he had learned about his insecurities and his need to control. He apologized for the pain he had caused her over the years, pain that had made her vulnerable to being involved with another man. He asked for another chance. Although they remained separated, his actions forced Anita to examine her own behaviors.

4. **Understand Anita.** Subsequent counseling sessions with Allen focused on Anita's character, lifestyle, and behavior. The goal here was to help Allen further appreciate Anita's gifts and contributions to his life and their marriage. Allen learned that he needed to be patient with Anita and that pursuing her and meeting her emotional needs would be the key in helping her leave Hugh and heal their marriage. He must not blame her and must not be defensive.

Allen told Anita that he wanted her to end the affair, that it was behavior he would not accept, but he also focused on how he could change himself and bring out Anita's best.

Counseling Anita: "Is This Really You?"

After I had counseled Allen individually for several weeks, Anita finally decided to join him. But first I had an individual session with her in which she strongly defended her thoughts on monogamy and her right to have close relationships with anyone she chose.

"Everyone, whether they're married or not, has a need from time to time to have a close relationship with a person of the opposite sex," Anita said. "I can go on the Internet and develop relationships with men, and women, for that matter, and not have it affect my marriage. And I would support Allen if he wanted to do the same thing. I'm mature enough to handle it."

Anita did say she planned to honor her husband's request to end her relationship with Hugh and to work on their marriage, but she wasn't ready to have Allen move back home yet.

The following two weeks went well. Allen started to let go of some of his control, and he began to rediscover his fun-loving spirit and spontaneous behavior that Anita once fell in love with. This affected Anita in a powerful and positive way. She quickly lost interest in her Internet relationships and began to focus on Allen again.

Allen and Anita's Chat Room

Allen and Anita's first joint counseling sessions centered around the strength of their first five years of marriage and how the last couple of weeks were a reflection of what they could recreate together. They could choose to focus on the hurt of her affair and his sex-line exploits, or they could focus on what had worked over the past two weeks and what had worked in the first five years of their marriage.

Anita and Allen also developed an agreement about relationships with people outside the marriage. For the first time, Anita acknowledged that she was hurt when Allen made calls to sex lines. They agreed they would not try to control what the other did on their own time, but each also would be responsible for not hurting the other with these relationships.

Nobody likes to be told what to do. But marriage partners still must be accountable to their spouses for their actions. They must understand that developing emotional relationships outside of marriage can be hurtful and can damage their marriage.

Allen and Anita's ability to work on their own behaviors was key to ending the affair and healing their marriage. Allen became less controlling and more emotionally involved in the marriage.

Anita let go of Hugh and other Internet relationships. She also forgave Allen for his urge to control, and she worked on not becoming angry and withdrawn from Allen when life didn't go smoothly.

Every marriage can be a strong one as long as each person wants to serve the other instead of becoming self-serving. Anita and Allen were able to turn their attitudes around so that the only chat room either needs is their living room.

But what if Anita desires to return to opposite-sex relationships over the Internet in the future? I told Anita during our last session that she must be open with Allen if she fell into that trap again. She agreed, and she told Allen that she would talk to him if she began slipping in that direction. Making that decision at this time, helped her see the value in making sure her actions reflected her values instead of the values of friends who were in bad marriages. Anita realized that it wasn't like her to have a value system based on her impulses.

Recap

Here is a review of other critical areas in the healing process of The Affair of the Future:

1. Allen and Anita began doing things together instead of Anita spending countless hours alone on the computer. They learned that their marriage could still be as exciting as it was during the first five years.
2. Allen forgave Anita instead of using the Cyber Affair against her when he became angry.
3. Anita began to understand the hurt she caused Allen during her Internet experience. She became more sensitive to his needs in their marriage.
4. Allen focused on Anita's gifts and beauty instead of her mistake.
5. Anita appreciated Allen's forgiveness and his willingness to give her the space she needed.

Chapter Eight
Healing and Reconciliation

༽ᘘᘘᘘᘘᘘᘘᘘᘘᘘᘘᘘᘘᘘ

An affair is like a heart attack. First, there's the discovery of the affair—a devastating shock to one, if not both, of the people in the marriage. As with the heart attack sufferer, once they've recovered from the trauma of the moment, they must heal the wounds and change their life patterns so the "heart attack" never occurs again, and they can have a healthy future. There needs to be continual rehabilitation if the marriage is to be restored, but it doesn't have to feel like rehabilitation. It can feel like renewal and regeneration, and it can be enjoyable and fulfilling. But it takes real focus and determination to take things slow and steady.

I have found that there are ten steps a couple must implement if they are to fully recover from an affair. The steps are presented here in the order that they must be done. When the husband and wife are at their best, all ten will work for them.

These ten steps are vital to the life of any marriage, regardless if there has been infidelity or not. Healing and reconciliation are regular exercises all marriages need.

1. Forgiveness

Forgiveness is the key to healing and reconciling a marriage damaged by an affair. In most instances, both people in the marriage must forgive each other.

Double-Life-Man affairs are usually the only ones in which forgiveness is a one-way street. The wife of a Double-Life Man usually has given the man everything he could have hoped for in a marriage, and she has nothing to apologize for. The marriage was damaged solely by the man's immaturity, and healing the marriage is completely dependent on the woman's ability to forgive her husband for the years he cheated on her.

Pleasers generally have a more difficult time forgiving than do Controllers. This is because Pleasers keep their emotions to themselves and may reach a point where they can't forgive at all. Controllers get angry more quickly, but they also are able to forgive more quickly.

Forgiveness is easiest when a passive person cheats on a controlling spouse. Controllers are extremely angry when the affair is discovered, but they quickly move on to repairing the marriage.

This was the case for a Controlling Woman-Passive Man couple I counseled. The man was able to move the reconciliation process along quickly because he immediately sought forgiveness after his four-year affair was exposed. He told his wife he was sorry for having the affair and for hurting her, and he asked for her forgiveness. He didn't try to justify his actions, as most adulterers do once their affair is discovered. He humbled himself right away. His wife didn't immediately forgive him, but his quick and sincere apology helped her do so over time because she could tell by his actions that he really was sorry and that he was serious about working on their marriage. The adulterer must clearly and openly ask for forgiveness.

Forgiveness is needed in every marriage for slights that may happen on a daily basis or for something as big as an affair. The capacity to forgive is a sign of emotional strength and maturity and is necessary for a healthy relationship. If couples are unable to forgive each other, their marriage will always be a struggle, as they will be hopelessly stuck in a sea of anger, self-protection, and victimization. Forgiveness frees couples and often brings them closer together than ever before.

2. Honesty

Honesty is destroyed the moment an affair starts. An affair depends on secrets, which lead to ongoing lies that build a wall of deceit around the affair. The adulterer's willingness to be honest is the only way to break down the wall, weaken the affair, and heal the marriage. Honesty brings accountability to the forefront and helps prevent further mistakes.

As the couple is healing and reconciling, they must practice honesty with each other at all times. There can be no room for lies, even "white lies" that are intended to protect loved ones from further hurts.

Talking about positive aspects of their marriage should account for 80 percent of their conversation with each other, while the remaining 20 percent should center on things that bother them about each other. Of course, it's difficult to see how 80 percent of their conversation can focus on the positive when they're trying to recover from the devastation of an affair. Both people will naturally want to focus on each other's shortcomings. But they must stay focused on the positive.

To do this, I ask each person to commit to saying at least five positive things to their spouse each day. Statements such as, "I'm sorry for all the pain I've caused you," "I enjoyed our time together tonight," " Thanks for being patient with me," "I want to be with you," "You look great in that dress today," or "Thanks for taking the kids to the mall." This exercise forces the couple to look for good things to say about the other and leads to more positive communication over time. They're no longer focusing on the things they don't like about their spouse.

Time should be set aside a couple of times a week solely for talking about the pain caused by the affair and about other negative subjects. This way the couple controls the affair, not the other way around.

Most couples healing from an affair worry when there is no communication. This is especially true for the spouse who wasn't in the affair. It's critical for both people to express their thoughts and to give each other reassurance. Through honesty, they can learn of each other's needs in marriage.

Honesty brings fullness and depth to a marriage that was previously hanging by a thread. It allows both people to grow, accept, and fall in love once again—or perhaps for the very first time.

3. Trust

Trust is the one aspect of a marriage that is most devastated by an affair. Countless individuals say to me, "How can I ever trust this person again?" But trust can be rebuilt if there is forgiveness and a return to honesty.

If the couple agrees that their marriage can't survive another affair—that another affair will result in certain divorce—then it's unlikely they'll obsess about the possibility of another affair. This helps the couple put one area of the trust issue behind them.

Trust seems easier to rebuild if the adulterer is truly remorseful and if his or her attitude shows that. If the adulterer shows sorrow, it gives the spouse a chance to believe again. When the adulterer's attitude is one of frustration, anger, and despair in returning to the marriage, it is difficult to rebuild trust. If the adulterer's attitude is sound, it is the spouse's role in marriage to forgive, to be honest, and to choose to trust. It will help them heal their life if they commit to this attitude.

Another key to regaining trust is celebrating the new strength in their marriage. The marriage withstood the ultimate attack of an affair. It wasn't fun or easy, but they survived. By focusing on the power of healing, forgiveness, and honesty, the couple can begin to realize that their trust for each other can tower to new heights. The couple's ability to give this sense of trust to each other may be greater now than ever before. They have learned how to hang on during the very worst of times and make a commitment to reconcile their love for each other.

4. Time

I have developed the Three Tiers of Time as a tool to helping struggling couples learn how to properly spend their time in marriage. The three tiers are Marriage Time, Family Time, and Individual Time. Each is important to healing a broken marriage.

For the couple to heal and reconcile properly, there must be a structure in place that allows them to spend time together with each other, their children, and their friends. They also need time alone. If the couple is not conscious about balancing their time, it can diminish the strength of the principles of forgiveness, honesty, and trust. Structured time for these relationships provides the opportunity for each spouse to see these concepts take root in the marriage.

Tier 1—Marriage Time—is the most important. It includes date nights, daily sharing, weekend excursions, and intimacy.

The couple must commit to spending one night a week alone together. Many couples develop a date night that is their night out alone regardless of what comes up. It doesn't have to be the same night every week, but it needs to happen once a week. It's wonderful to see a couple choose to keep their date night instead of canceling because of a board meeting, social gathering, or family activity. The marriage needs to be nourished first.

When a couple prioritizes their time rightly, it helps them see how much they value spending time together. It not only gives them something to look forward to, but it also helps them feel secure in their reconciliation process.

To give a date night even more strength, the spouses should take turns planning the night. It doesn't have to be expensive or fancy. It is the thought and the commitment that counts.

Far too often, a couple begins scheduling date nights, but fails to continue doing so by the second month. Something always comes up to alter the process, such as a child's game or recital. They should attend the game or recital, but they should reschedule the date for later in the week. It's that important.

The couple also must spend fifteen to thirty minutes together every day or night in noninterrupted conversation. These should be intimate, nonsexual times for talking about whatever they want. Active listening is the key for these times. As a couple heals from an affair, part of this time can be used to assess how each person feels about the process.

Occasionally, the spouse who didn't have the affair must discuss his or her feelings of pain and hurt from the affair. This process must be handled delicately. The person who had the affair should give reassurance of his or her commitment to the marriage, while the other spouse must offer ongoing forgiveness.

THE THREE TIERS OF TIME

Tier 1 : Marriage Time

Date Nights   Weekend Excursions
Daily Sharing   Intimacy

Tier 2 : Family Time

Family   Family
Traditions   Discussions

Tier 3 : Individual Time

Friends   Hobbies

© Todd K. Mulliken, 1995

The third part of Tier 1 calls for the couple to take mini-vacations or overnight excursions alone every two months. This is especially true for the first year or two after an affair has ended. These times alone allow the couple to have extended, uninterrupted time to be with each other sharing their love. This environment also allows forgiveness, honesty, and trust to really take hold in the marriage. A bed and breakfast, a family-owned cabin, or a modest hotel are all good places for these excursions.

Tier 1 is the most crucial of the Three Tiers of Time. It sets the tone for the marriage, family, and individual environments. Many people neglect Tier 1, and that's why their marriages often fall into trouble.

Tier 2 involves planning time for the family, if there is one. The children of families that are recovering from affairs are also recovering. It's likely that the children were neglected during the affair, especially by the adulterer. The children were emotionally starved during the affair, and they desperately need their family life to return.

One of the best ways to rebuild family security is through family traditions. One particularly healthy tradition is a weekly time to get together as a family for fifteen to thirty minutes to discuss any important matters. It's critical that the parents be mature enough to handle these meetings, so they don't become blame sessions. They need to be structured so that anyone can talk about anything they would like related to the family. This can be especially helpful for a family that is healing from an affair. It gives the children a chance to disclose emotions if they want to.

Other family traditions could be going to brunch after church every other week, going to the local bagel shop every Saturday morning, or having Sunday dinner together.

Children generally look forward to family traditions, especially if they are planned so they don't miss any time with their friends. When the children are in their teens, the tradition may have to occur every other week, but it's essential that it occurs on a regular basis.

Tier 2 provides a vehicle that ensures a sense of commitment to the importance of family cohesiveness and intimacy, which helps children grow emotionally and enhances their self-image. It gives the children a sense of a safe place to which they belong, and they feel respected and loved.

Tier 3 is reserved for individual time, whether it's alone, with friends or with hobbies. Individual time is especially important for adulterers as they return to family life. They feel disconnected and are still reeling from the loss of their affair. The Passive and the Pleaser adulterers especially struggle with this.

The Three Tiers of Time work only if two rules are followed:

1. No time can be spent alone if Tiers 1 and 2 are not in place on a regular basis.
2. Individual time must be equally distributed. Typically, early in the reconciliation stage, one night per week for each person is helpful to allow some space for each person.

Many marriages have the tiers tipped upside down, with the spouses spending much more time *away* from each other than they do *with* each other. The beautiful part of staying focused on these tiers is that it builds maturity in the area that needs the most help— the marriage. As the marriage matures, the family builds intimacy and stability, and both partners can feel free to do things on their own versus feeling guilty if they want to get out of the house by themselves.

5. Intimacy

The return of intimacy to a marriage that is healing from an affair depends completely on whether there is forgiveness, a return to honesty and trust, and a serious attempt to abide by the Three Tiers of Time.

Usually, at least one of the marriage partners struggles with affection and lovemaking during the healing process because of the loss of love before and during the affair. But, eventually, intimacy and lovemaking will return naturally, if both people are active in giving to each other.

Over time, adulterers rediscover their security and stability in marriage and family life, and the result is renewed intimacy. Spouses of adulterers may be sexually aggressive early in the healing process in order to prove their self-worth, then may back off due to hurt and anger. They may continue to be erratic in intimacy for a time because of their insecurities about the affair.

Personalities play a big role in the return of intimacy. Controllers will be sexual more quickly because they are impulsive and generally lack emotional attachment. Pleasers will be more tentative and cautious because of the hurt and resentment they carry internally.

For intimacy to return, both people must be open to subtle signs of affection from each other. This will lead to deeper levels of intimacy in foreplay and lovemaking. Both partners must be patient during this process.

In some cases, intimacy in the form of lovemaking returns immediately, which greatly helps the couple with forgiveness, honesty, and trust. Sex is powerful. But in the majority of cases, intimacy returns only after the marriage and family life have become secure and stable again. If the couple strives to create this atmosphere in their home, then intimacy will return and blossom.

6. Friendships

During an affair, the friendships couples once shared can change drastically or even disappear. Adulterers often isolate themselves from family and friends, while their spouses often get closer to these friends during the affair and while it is being exposed. Obviously, this creates uncomfortable situations and usually changes the nature of the friendships.

These friends were part of the family's life before the affair started, and it's imperative that the couple try to renew these relationships, regardless of how the friends were affected by the affair. But this should happen only if both spouses agree to rekindling the friendships.

It's easier to return to friendships when it was the controlling spouse who had the affair because Controllers usually don't care a lot about what other people think of them. They're able to move on with life quickly. Renewing friendships is especially difficult for Pleaser adulterers because they constantly worry about what other people think. In these cases, the friends may have to take steps to rekindle the friendship and reassure them that they are still loved.

The couple's ability to reconnect with special friends is critical to the healing and reconciliation process. It creates an environment in which the couple can see that healing is not only wonderful in marriage, but it is also a joy with friends. These friends likely will create a powerful feeling of restoration to the marriage in a loving and accepting manner.

7. Personal Growth

All of the steps mentioned so far deal with the marriage relationship. But personal growth is as important as any of the first six steps. It's critical that both husband and wife continue to work on their self-image, understand their own personality, and identify and set personal goals in their lives.

Controllers must learn to think about others before acting. They must pay attention to how they speak to their spouses. Pleasers must learn to think about themselves more. They shouldn't worry about what they say, but rather learn how to express their thoughts more often.

In the case of extreme Controllers and extreme Pleasers, changing their personalities is critical to their marriage. If they don't work on their own personal growth throughout the healing and reconciliation process, their capacity to do these things will be greatly hindered.

In addition to working on their own growth, each partner must accept the other as they learn about themselves. Change occurs slowly. A person's innate personality never changes completely, but the refinements emphasized in counseling are areas that will help each person become more fit for marriage and family life.

8. Attitude Check

The attitude each person has toward the marriage will determine how quickly—or, if—they will heal and reconcile.

Most couples going through an affair feel hurt and betrayed. These emotions often produce an attitude of "You owe me," or "What have you done for me lately?" This type of thinking leads to self-protection, individualism, and an eventual divorce. Both people must make sure these thoughts don't control their actions.

The couple must check their attitude regularly. Adulterers can't continue to blame the affair on their spouses and their shortcomings. The spouses of adulterers can't obsess about the affair and their anger.

I had one case in which a couple had spent eighteen months thinking only about what their spouse wasn't doing for them. When they came to me for their first counseling session, I asked them to change their attitudes and think, "What can I do for my spouse today?" Three months later they had completely changed how they looked at each other and were well on their way to healing their marriage.

Attitude is a choice. If a couple is serious about saving their marriage, they must get control of their attitudes. They must focus on the positive aspects of each other, not on feeling victimized and short-changed in life. This means compromising their emotions a bit and concentrating on the hope of forgiveness and reconciliation.

9. Sharing a Vision

A Bible verse, Proverbs 29:18, says, "Where there is no vision, the people perish . . ." (KJV). This is true for a marriage as well. A couple healing from an affair must capture a vision for their future together, including family, financial, career, and relationship goals.

This may be hard to address at first because both people are focusing on forgiveness and rebuilding honesty and trust. Sometimes they are just trying to get through the day. But they must discuss some of their dreams and goals in order to become unified in their commitment to the future together. Sharing a vision of their future reassures the spouse of the adulterer that another affair will not happen. A vision of the future helps adulterers restructure their thoughts toward the family and the reality of life together.

One problem is that affairs often are based on a future together. The two people having an affair often plan a life together. Pleaser women, especially, are great at planning and romanticizing about the future. In an affair, they often feel they have found the man of their dreams. He would have the same vision of the future as she, and he would make her dreams come true. A Pleaser woman often takes longer to return to a future vision with her husband because her "dreams" were shattered by the end of the affair. Husbands of these women need to be especially sensitive to this and to take things slowly.

It's exciting to plan and share a vision together, but the process is not static. It's ongoing and can change over time. This process, however, provides stability and enhances the couple's healing process and their ability to become stronger as a team than ever before.

10. Renewal of Vows

One of the most powerful experiences a couple that is healing from an affair can have is renewing their marriage vows. Whether it's formal or informal, renewing vows brings reassurance and security to spouses of adulterers, while adulterers gain a sense of structure and direction in their marriage and family.

I've had couples go as far as formally renewing their vows in a church with a priest and important family members and friends in the pews. It was like a second wedding. I've also had couples spontaneously decide to renew their vows in front of me in my office. However it's done, renewing the commitment to each other is an important final step to reconciling a marriage that has been damaged by an affair. It's a wonderful way to get a fresh start.

A couple can renew their vows immediately after reconciliation, but it will have more impact if they wait six to twelve months afterward. This assures that the reconciliation is mature.

The process of renewing vows is not only powerful for the couple, but it's also influential on the children, family, and friends who knew about the affair. It gives the children a true sense of stability. People love to see renewal and hope.

Chapter Nine
Prevention

⟨∭⟩

Most people who have affairs eventually regret it. They find that the pain and confusion that accompany an affair outweigh the passion, desire, and love the affair temporarily creates in their lives. The hurt felt by loved ones affected by the affair is immeasurable. There is nothing more damaging to a marriage than an affair.

With that in mind, it's important for all couples, including those who strongly believe that their marriage is immune to infidelity, to learn how to prevent affairs. There are five specific ways couples can prevent an affair from happening. Each is of equal importance, and all five are needed for a couple to make themselves as affair-proof as possible.

UNDERSTAND YOUR PERSONALITY

Controllers

Controllers face two major issues that make them susceptible to affairs: They often don't know where to draw the line in their relationships with the opposite sex, and they are naturally self-centered.

Controlling Men usually begin having boundary problems with women during their teen years. They often cheat on their girlfriends, or they are close to other girls in nonromantic relationships. They use these relationships to fill insecurities due to a lack of emotional attachment to their father. This pattern usually continues into marriage, but by that time the stakes are considerably higher. It's one thing to dump one girlfriend for another. It's quite another to enter an affair and risk ruining a marriage, especially one that involves children.

If a Controlling Man is going to have an affair, it most likely will happen at work where he is in a position of power. These kinds of affairs are more likely to happen in certain industries, such as politics or traveling sales, and in certain relationships, such as boss/secretary or professional/client.

Affairs commonly occur in the airline industry. A typical affair happens between a Controlling male pilot and a Pleaser female flight attendant. They find overnight layovers in cities far away from their hometowns perfect opportunities to pursue their relationship.

Most pilots and flight attendants don't have affairs, but they work in a profession in which their work environment leaves lots of room for Controlling Men to engage in infidelity. It's essential for Controlling Men to be aware of their environment and their relationships with other women. They need to set strict boundaries. They need to save all their best for their wives.

Controlling Women can have similar boundary problems with members of the opposite sex. Sometimes the Controlling Woman who is most vulnerable to an affair is unmarried or is in between marriages. She has a hard time settling down with men. She's impulsive, restless, easily distracted, and noncommitted. She sees something she wants, and she goes after it, regardless of the costs.

How do Controllers keep themselves from becoming vulnerable to affairs? They need to keep themselves from one-on-one encounters with the opposite sex. One of my clients refuses to do anything alone with any woman other than his wife, even if it appears to be an innocent lunch with a family friend or an all-business meeting over dinner with a client. He always tries to have at least one other person with them for these meetings. If that's impossible, then he makes sure the meeting is held at his office or some other place where a personal relationship is more difficult to start. He doesn't want to take any chance of another affair developing in his life.

Controllers can also help themselves by developing deep relationships with friends of their own gender who have strong marriages. These friends will often become role models to the Controllers, holding them accountable for their actions and helping them mature.

Selfishness also can leave Controllers vulnerable to affairs. Controllers sometimes struggle with intimate relationships because of their inability to love. They speak and act before they think. This is both their strength and their weakness. In business, such decision-making and conflict-resolution skills are essential. But Controllers can struggle in intimate relationships because they don't think enough about how their actions will affect their spouse. They are too focused on their own thoughts and feelings.

To break this pattern, Controllers must learn to think of others first. The more they can do this, the less likely they will be to step out into an affair or force their lonely spouse to be vulnerable to one.

Pleasers

Pleasers were often controlled growing up at home and again later in marriage. They may try to finally assert themselves by getting involved in an affair. They say they're tired of being controlled by everyone in their life, and they have found someone who makes them truly happy. But they're often being controlled in the affair, also. They may not think that's true, because the Controller with whom they are having the affair controls in a subtle way and makes the Pleaser feel valued and respected.

Pleasers need to understand that they are easily controlled and that they need to assert themselves and stand up for their rights early in marriage. If they wait fifteen years into marriage to take these steps, it's more likely they'll have an affair or choose divorce instead of changing themselves.

They can learn to assert themselves by beginning to "talk their thoughts." They should act like a Controller and not worry about what they're going to say. Pleasers have been shut down for so long that they don't know how to speak their minds, but they can learn.

BUILD SELF-IMAGE

It's rare that a person with a healthy self-image will have an affair. In almost every affair, the adulterer is either extremely frustrated with marriage or suffers from a character flaw. They also struggle with their self-image and lack direction and meaning in life. An affair may give them temporary purpose and fulfillment, but it won't fulfill lifetime dreams and goals. While some people intentionally set out to have an affair, most adulterers struggle with a marriage that has been flat for more than ten years before they consider becoming unfaithful. They get to the point that they don't care if they hurt their spouse because they feel they deserve happiness. But in almost every case, the adulterer didn't set out to have an affair. It "just happened."

When people feel frustrated or stuck in marriage, they need to do two things: They need to talk with their spouse and try to work on the marriage together. If this doesn't work, they need to find a counselor. If one spouse isn't interested in counseling, the other should go anyway. Many times one spouse will recognize a need for help—it's usually the woman—and the other spouse will not want to go to counseling. The dissenting spouse will eventually attend, sometimes by giving in to their spouse's persistence. If couples would turn to good marriage counseling when they begin to feel some frustration, more than half of the affairs in America would never occur.

Second, the couple must start working on their self-image. They can use the Three-Step Guide to a Healthy Self-Image or a similar tool that will help them understand their past, assess their present situation, and set goals for their future.

Double-Life Men especially benefit from building their self-image. This is hard because the Double-Life Man rarely thinks he has a problem. He's successful at work, his home life is fine, and he's in a great affair. If he works on his self-image early in life, however, he may never become vulnerable to an affair, which could ruin everything he loves about his life. Building his self-image and understanding how he developed Double-Life tendencies may be a less-painful option. But most Double-Life Men think they can solve their problems on their own.

Building a good self-image is an ongoing process that should be regularly evaluated. Goals, directions, and thoughts change often in life. Assessing self-image on a regular basis helps fulfill dreams and prevents adultery.

RESOLVING MARITAL CONFLICT SUCCESSFULLY

Couples usually lose love for each other because of their inability to take care of each other in conflicts. They see each other's worst attributes during these discussions. If these conflicts go unresolved, or are controlled by the Controller in the marriage, the Passive partner may become vulnerable to an affair. The Pleaser gets worn down, frustrated, and sees no end to these types of conflicts and how they are handled. The Controller gets irritated with the Pleaser's silence and withdrawal in conflict. They feel as if nothing is ever resolved.

A mature couple handles conflict well. They don't verbally abuse each other, and they don't give each other the silent treatment. They make an effort to understand why the other feels bad, and they try to reach an amicable decision. Every marriage has conflicts. The key to maintaining love in marriage is handling conflict well.

Here are some basic keys to successfully handling conflict in marriage:

1. Listen to each other.
2. Respect each other's opinion.
3. Talk using "I" statements. Sentences that begin with "You" are unacceptable. They are blame-oriented.
4. Don't judge your spouse's opinion.
5. Clearly identify why you feel the way you do.
6. Do not yell or scream. Talk with a respectful tone to each other.
7. If you are a Controller, let the Pleaser do the talking for once. Do not interrupt!

8. If you are a Pleaser, do not hide your opinion. Say what you need to say and assert it in love.
9. Try to reach a point of mutual agreement on the conflict.
10. If you cannot agree, reach a compromise that both can live with.

How do you handle conflict in your marriage? Are you the Controller? The Pleaser? How many of the ten keys to handling conflict in marriage do you follow as a couple? You will have a much more satisfying marriage if you can work through your conflicts with grace and understanding. Couples need to save their very best efforts for when conflicts arise. Unfortunately, most couples dump all of their pent-up anger and pain, plus their frustrations of that particular day, on their spouse during conflict.

BRING OUT EACH OTHER'S BEST

People usually see the best in their partner during courtship. It's during this part of the relationship that they have the grace to forgive errors, accept annoying habits, resolve conflict swiftly, truly give to each other, and the romance is alive and thriving.

It's difficult to sustain this kind of relationship, but it's important that couples try to do so on a daily basis. Following are my ten ways to Bring Out Each Other's Best in marriage. A worksheet is included in Appendix B in the back of the book. As you read these, think about which ones you're currently doing for your spouse and which ones you're neglecting.

Ten Ways to Bring Out Each Other's Best
1. **Being *accepted* for who I am.** More than half of all Americans desire this most from their mate. People can easily become vulnerable to an affair if they constantly feel they don't measure up to their spouse's ideals.

Many people feel they lose their identity in marriage. This is often the case when people do not feel accepted for who they are. They mold themselves to become a person that fits the attitudes of their spouse. This will never work. People need to feel free to be themselves and to be accepted as they are.

Some behaviors, of course, are unacceptable in marriage. These include adultery, alcoholism and drug abuse, and physical, emotional, and sexual abuse. People with these problems need to resolve them in order to be fit for marriage. Beyond these severe problems, however, people need to adopt a general attitude of acceptance for their spouse. An attitude of acceptance creates an environment where romance can flourish because both people feel free to be themselves and to know they are loved. An affair would be one of the last things on their mind.

2. Receiving *affirmation* for what I've done. I often tell my clients, "Listen to what you say to your spouse for one day." They'll find that more than 80 percent of what they say is either critical or non-affirming. It's amazing how quickly respect can leave a marriage. Many people hold onto the adage that "Love is never having to say you're sorry." Or they'll say, "Of course I love you. I married you, didn't I?"

It's easy for couples to stop acknowledging each other for the contributions they are making to the family on a daily basis. My goal with couples is to help them turn their discussions into 80 percent affirmations. Criticism needs to be handled honestly and with care. Criticism should be the exception, not the rule.

3. Managing our *conflicts* well. Pleasers will generally put this as their number one or number two priority. Pleasers struggle with conflict because to them, conflict means they have failed in their role of making their spouse happy. It's a great attitude to have in general, but it would be better for the marriage if the Controller took this stance instead. Controllers don't mind conflict. They like to express their views, and they want their Pleaser spouse to do the same. Controllers must manage conflict to keep their spouse happy.

4. Be *honest* with me. Couples who are recovering from an affair tend to make this their number-one choice. Nothing is more discouraging in marriage than believing you are being lied to.

Couples can talk honestly with each other if they "talk their thoughts." It helps them be open and more transparent with each other, and it challenges them to be accountable for their thoughts. Thoughts that are degrading to a spouse occur less often if people are challenged to talk about what's on their minds.

5. Physical *intimacy.* Affection and lovemaking are integral parts of any marriage. A classic trademark of a marriage being attacked by an affair is one in which sex has been eliminated from daily life. This is almost always the case if the man's having the affair. Men usually need sex more than women. If the man isn't initiating sex nearly as often as he used to, it may be because he's getting it somewhere else.

When a woman is having an affair, she may continue to have regular sex with her husband until she's fully committed to her new partner. Then she will stop having sex in marriage.

Here are some ways a couple can create lasting intimacy in their marriage:

1. *Understand what your spouse loves most about affection.* Affection means different things to different people. Some people love physical affection such as massages, while others prefer more verbal signs of affection, such as compliments: "I love you," "Thank you," or notes and cards. Don't go by what you need for affection. Learn what brings out the best in your spouse.

2. *Affection needs spontaneity and planning.* People must think about their spouses more often. Plan a time when you give your spouse a backrub or write a thoughtful card. Let affection be natural as well. There is nothing more romantic than spontaneous endearment and touch. Look for these opportunities, and don't put them off because you are out of time or are not in the mood. Be open to spontaneity.

3. *Take time to make love and take your time in doing so.* Most couples who are struggling with their marriage also are struggling with their sex life. It's almost always the same story: The men aren't getting enough, and the women feel their

husbands are too demanding sexually. The men complain that their wives are never in the mood, and the women complain that when they do make love, it is over before they really get in the mood.

To resolve this, the couple must make love—preferably three or four times a week—and they must take their time doing it. Women are clearly more interested in foreplay and afterplay than they are with intercourse. This is where men make their biggest mistake. Men want to proceed immediately to intercourse and have an orgasm. They're asleep thirty seconds later. To satisfy his wife, a man must be sensitive to her and have at least fifteen minutes of foreplay. This time should center on the woman and her need for arousal and stimulation. She may even choose to have an orgasm during this stage.

Intercourse should last at least fifteen minutes, if the woman wants it to last that long. The goal here is mutual climax, but it's difficult, so don't worry if it's not achieved. After intercourse, it's critical for the couple to relax together and to be close for a period of time. Some women choose to climax again during this phase. Make lovemaking an encounter. Take the time to truly show care and love for each other. The key for great lovemaking is in the man's ability to be sensitive, caring, and romantic. If he's not, the woman may not even take the time to make time.

6. Being actively *listened* to. People often hear each other but don't actively listen to each other. Controllers will nod their heads while focusing on what they're going to say when it's their turn to talk. Pleasers will shut down and tune out while the Controller talks. A critical part of listening involves drawing out the other person and trying to understand why they have their opinion on a certain matter. Controllers need to take the time to listen, while Pleasers need to be open about what they are hearing and to give opinions about it. Active listening is a technique. It takes practice. It's an amazingly intimate capability when it's done well. The people who are listened to feel actively empowered because they feel they are heard and understood. Even if they are not agreed with, they feel respected and important. Save your very best listening skills for your marriage.

7. Being involved in *parenting* our children. Many women will put this in their top two or three priority. It brings fulfillment to their hearts when the father of their children is nurturing and is an active part of the children's lives. As long as a man works hard, his wife will care more about how involved he is in their children's lives and not so much about how much money he makes. Men are now doing a much better job in this area than they did in past generations.

Men also feel fulfilled when they see their wives involved in their children's lives, although they usually don't list it in their top five. The family will be stronger if both parents are actively involved in parenting. The love of children and the sense of family stability is often what brings the adulterer back home.

8. *Planning* dates and time together. One of the best ways to avoid an affair is to never have time to have one. A marriage will struggle unless the couple shares time alone as a couple and together as a family. They should follow the Three Tiers of Time. It's important to plan together. Spend fifteen minutes together every Sunday night to plan the next week or two, including who's going to find the baby-sitter. The couple that has enough structure in their marriage to plan dates and times together without letting the structure ruin their spontaneity has really arrived.

9. *Protecting* me from my spouse's anger and criticism. People who are exposed to a great deal of anger and criticism from their spouse often become vulnerable to affairs. Pleasers are often shut down by anger. Controllers tend to express their thoughts, whether positive or negative, leaving their Passive spouse subject to their outward anger and frustration. Controllers don't mind if Pleasers are angry or critical. They just want to know what's on their spouse's mind. Whether it's positive or negative is less of an issue with the

Controller. Controllers really need to watch how they talk because Pleasers are extremely sensitive to anger and criticism.

Pleasers don't really need to protect their spouse from their anger and criticism. Rather, they need to work on expressing it more. The Pleaser shouldn't be looking for opportunities to be angry, but rather learn how to express their anger with respect if the feelings are there. Most Pleasers rate this area as one of the top ways their spouse can help them the most. When the Controller protects the Pleaser from their anger and critical nature, it frees the Pleaser to express more opinions and feel safe and loved in the marriage. This concept of working on their anger and criticism is the most important area for the Controller to address in marriage.

10. Emotionally *pursuing* me. Most women say this is important in bringing out their best. Men are usually good at this during courtship, but stop doing it after marriage. They settle into patterns of silence, withdrawal, and the pursuit of other interests. Men tend to throw their identity into work. They pursue their vocations and stop pursuing their wives. Here are some ways for men to pursue their wives:

1. Think about her more often, and let her know that you do.
2. Spend time actively listening to her each day.
3. Leave signs, such as notes, little cards, and Post-Its that say endearing things. I often tell men to go to a card shop, buy ten cards, and give one card to their wives once a week for ten weeks.
4. Give lots of affection without sex attached to it.
5. Be open about what's on your mind. Share your thoughts as they develop.

In one of my cases, a Pleaser Woman was feeling unloved by her Controller husband. When I talked to him, I could tell he loved her a great deal, but he didn't show it in his actions. He was always telling her what to do and how to do things. He was acting more like her parent than her husband. Once he understood this and began using all five of the above tactics regularly, their marriage turned around in a month.

If men continue to pursue in marriage, then their wives won't want to have an affair. The only time a woman doesn't want to be pursued by her husband is when she's in an affair or was just in one. At this point, she generally wants to heal slowly and not be pursued. Women pursue their husbands well in marriage. The relationship is always on their minds. The key is for the man to think more about his wife.

PLANNING FOR SUCCESS: GROWING TOGETHER VS. GROWING APART

Many couples tell me, "We have grown apart." In four of the five most common types of affairs in America today, this feeling is always the case. The only exception is the Double-Life Man Affair, which occurs solely because of the man's emotional problems. The wife has done nothing wrong, and she and her husband could actually appear to be growing together while the man is in the affair. In the other four types of affairs, the couple has usually grown apart because their relationship is in a rut, and they are off doing their own thing. They're not resolving conflicts together, they're not pursuing each other, they're not bringing out each other's best, and they're not planning together. They are simply existing together.

Planning for success in marriage involves ongoing communication about each other's dreams and goals. The visioning process is critical here as well. Couples do a pretty good job with this while they are courting. But when they get into the daily routine of marriage, they can easily lose their planning ideas. One of the greatest strengths in the affair is that the two individuals share their dreams and hopes for the future. It is usually somewhat delusional, but they do it.

Are you growing together as a couple or are you growing apart? Planning for success involves action and commitment.

A Message of Hope

Infidelity is a disease that is causing great havoc in America today. It destroys marriages, tears families apart, and adversely affects children for a lifetime. But like most diseases, it can be prevented through education, awareness, and other proactive measures. And most people can recover to live fulfilling lives, even if they are afflicted by the disease of infidelity, whether they are the adulterer or the spouse of one.

The two keys to preventing affairs are awareness and understanding. We, as a society, can make great strides toward preventing affairs if we understand that infidelity is common in America and that all of us could be vulnerable to an affair under the right circumstances. We can't delude ourselves and pretend that affairs happen only on television and among the morally corrupt. Affairs affect people from all socio-economic classes, ages, personalities, and family backgrounds. About 50 percent of all marriages in America are affected by infidelity. It's vital that everyone understands that infidelity is common and that affairs should not be taken lightly. They are extremely powerful. They provide things everyone desires: passion, physical excitement, and emotional satisfaction.

I believe fewer people would be tempted to have an affair if the disease of infidelity was talked about openly in our society. Infidelity draws much of its strength from its mysterious and secretive nature. This allure of affairs can be significantly weakened by taking the mystery out of them and by showing people ways to prevent infidelity and ways to recover if there is an affair.

Affairs can also be prevented if we understand why they happen and then take steps to fix the root of the problem. Eighty percent of women have affairs because they are dissatisfied with their marriage, while 80 percent of men have them because of an emotional problem that developed in childhood.

People must understand themselves and their spouses. By taking your "emotional temperature" on a regular basis, you can more easily keep your sense of meaning and direction in life and see when you or your spouse is more vulnerable to having an affair.

A regular run-through of Steps Two and Three in my Three-Step Guide to a Healthy Self-Image is a good check-up. Couples can do their regular check-ups together by evaluating their Three Tiers of Time, along with how they are bringing out each other's best. There's constant change during the life of a marriage, so the importance of a couple monitoring their vital signs cannot be emphasized enough. Understanding yourself and your spouse will greatly diminish the chances that your marriage will be threatened by infidelity.

What if you've already been touched by an affair? Don't give up hope, and don't think divorce is your only option. By taking the right steps, you can heal your marriage and again move on with a fulfilling life.

Healing and reconciling a marriage takes time and patience. It also takes a lot of work by both people in the marriage. Both people must make a concerted effort to heal themselves and to make the marriage work. Just as it takes two to make the commitment to marriage on the wedding day, it takes two to find the way out of marriage's darkest period. And once you've successfully navigated through that period together, you'll be an inspiration to your children, family, and friends. They will have seen your hearts, minds, and souls change, and they'll learn that forgiveness is preferred over divorce.

A Note from the Author

One thing that has strengthened my marriage with Laura has been our involvement in small groups with other couples. These times of Bible study, fellowship and, sharing have strengthened the bond of love in our marriage as we have shared our joys and sorrows.

None of the more than twenty couples we've befriended in these groups over the last ten years have divorced. They have chosen to grow together in a nurturing environment with others who value their relationship with God. I urge you to get involved in a local place of worship where such house groups are offered and learn where you and your spouse fit in.

I would also like to offer my services to speak at your church, place of business, school, or college about the state of affairs in our country. I enjoy sharing ways we can strengthen our families and avoid, or heal from, marriage's darkest season.

Appendix A
Three-Step Guide
to a Healthy Self-Image

Step One:
Understanding How Your Self-Image Was Shaped by Your Past

    a. In my years as a child and as an adolescent, what messages did I hear about myself from my parents, siblings, and friends?

    b. What shaped my self-image the most? My parents and family life? My friends? My grades? My dating relationships? My jobs? Something else?

    c. Entering adult life, how did I view myself?

    d. After understanding my past, what unhealthy patterns do I need to change?

Step Two:
Define Your Current Purpose and Meaning in Life

    a. Do I have a sense of direction in my life?

    b. Do I go through periods of boredom and frustration with my life?

    c. Do I think about what I want to accomplish in my life?

Step Three:
Set Goals in the Areas of Your Life in Which You Lack Direction

In which of these areas do you lack direction?

    a. Your relationship with God and your involvement in church

b. Your relationship with your spouse

c. Your relationships with your current family or your family of origin

d. Your work or career path

e. Your financial situation

f. Your physical health (diet, exercise, etc.)

g. Your social life (friendships with others)

Appendix B
How to Bring Out My Best

⊙⟋ⱮⱮⱮ⟍⊙

The following is a list of things your partner can do to bring out your best. Order them from 1 through 10, with 1 being the area that you feel will be most important to bring out your best. They're listed in alphabetical order.

____ Being *accepted* for who I am
____ Receiving *affirmation* for what I've done
____ Managing our *conflicts* well
____ Being *honest* with me
____ Physical *intimacy*
____ Being actively *listened* to
____ Being involved in *parenting* our children
____ *Planning* dates and time together
____ *Protecting* me from his/her anger and criticism
____ Emotionally *pursuing* me

Todd K. Mulliken, 1995 ©

To order additional copies of:

The State of Affairs

send $11.95 plus $3.95 shipping and handling to:

Books, Etc.
PO Box 1406
Mukilteo, WA 98275

or have your credit card ready and call:

(800) 917-BOOK